D1103646

PRAISE FOR PAUL GRIMES
AND *THE FACTS OF LIFE*

"Just what the consumer needs: a clear and practical guide to how much and what type of life insurance you need — in plain language. Author Paul Grimes not only untangles this complex subject but even manages to make it entertaining!"

— Normand Pépin, F.S.A., F.C.I.A., Executive Vice-President, Life Subsidiaries and Vice-President and General Manager, Individual Insurance and Annuities, Industrial Alliance Insurance and Financial Services

"Paul has made the often complex subject of life insurance simple, readable, and fun."

— Jim Rogers, MBA, CFP, RFP, CHFC Chairman, The Rogers Group Financial Advisors Ltd., Past Chairman, Canadian Association of Insurance and Financial Advisors

"Books on financial planning aren't new, but when Certified Financial Planner professionals publish their considerable expertise, they elevate awareness and recognition of this growing profession to the benefit of all."

— Don Johnston, President, Financial Planners Standards Council

THE FACTS OF LIFE

HOW TO BUILD WEALTH AND PROTECT YOUR ASSETS WITH LIFE INSURANCE

PAUL GRIMES
WITH SUSAN GOLDBERG

Published in 2002 by
Stoddart Publishing Co. Limited
895 Don Mills Road, 400-2 Park Centre, Toronto, Canada M3C 1W3
PMB 128, 4500 Witmer Estates, Niagara Falls, New York 14305-1386

www.stoddartpub.com

To order Stoddart books please contact General Distribution Services
In Canada Tel. (416) 213-1919   Fax (416) 213-1917
Email cservice@genpub.com
In the United States Toll-free tel. 1-800-805-1083 Toll-free fax 1-800-481-6207
Email gdsinc@genpub.com

10   9   8   7   6   5   4   3   2   1

National Library of Canada Cataloguing in Publication Data
Grimes, Paul
The facts of life: how to build wealth and protect your assets with life insurance
ISBN 0-7737-6235-3
1. Insurance, Life — Canada.   I. Goldberg, Susan   II. Title.
HG9010.G74   2002   368.32'00971   C2001-903430-X

U.S. Cataloging-in-Publication Data Available from the Library of Congress
ISBN 0-7737-6235-3

The author, in his capacity as an executive of the Industrial Alliance Group of Companies, is responsible for development, management, and sales in Ontario of Industrial Alliance life insurance and investment products. However, the opinions and recommendations expressed in this book are exclusively his and do not necessarily represent those of the Industrial Alliance Group of Companies.

Cover Design: Angel Guerra
Text design and typesetting: Kinetics Design & Illustration

THE CANADA COUNCIL | LE CONSEIL DES ARTS
FOR THE ARTS | DU CANADA
SINCE 1957 | DEPUIS 1957

We acknowledge for their financial support of our publishing program the Canada Council, the Ontario Arts Council, and the Government of Canada through the Book Publishing Industry Development Program (BPIDP).

Printed and bound in Canada

For Denise, Fraser, and Spencer

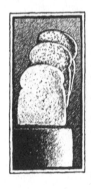

CONTENTS

Acknowledgements

IN January 2000 my family was enjoying the dawn of a new millennium in Florida. I had used some of the vacation as a time to catch up on reading, and one of the books I had brought along on the trip was David Cork and Susan Lightstone's *The Pig and the Python*. As I closed the book, I turned to my wife, Denise, and commented, "Someone should write a book like this on life insurance." Denise looked me in the eye and asked the obvious question: "Why not you?"

Well, that was (almost) all the encouragement I needed. Two years later, and here it is: *The Facts of Life: How to Build Wealth and Protect Your Assets with Life Insurance*.

In my twenty years in the life insurance industry, and in my seminars and speaking engagements, I have always tried to create simple explanations for complex situations. This approach is the backbone of *The Facts of Life*.

The goal of this book is simple: to provide Canadians with an easy-to-read guide to life insurance. For most Canadians, life insurance is a difficult product to understand and relate to. Given that insurance is, well, looked upon as a necessary evil, I decided to "humanize" it, explaining the various products and concepts in story form — the tale of a typical Canadian family. Susan Goldberg and I have created fictional characters, but the insurance products, facts, and circumstances these characters face are real. You may in fact face similar circumstances.

Many people have aided Susan and me in our work. We'd like to thank Normand Pépin, executive vice-president, Life Subsidiaries vice-president, and general manager Individual Insurance and Annuities, of the Industrial Alliance Life Insurance Company, who immediately recognized the value of this work and provided support for it. Don Bastian and Sue Sumeraj, our editors at Stoddart, shepherded this book through from proposal to finished product, and Ryan St. Onge, our publicist, offered his energy and optimism. We thank Janice Weaver for a thorough and thoughtful copy edit. David Cork and Susan Lightstone were among our biggest cheerleaders, and we'd like to thank Susan especially for introducing us to each other and for her generous guidance on the proposal. Ted Cadsby, Gordon Pape, and Gail Vaz-Oxlade listened and offered advice and encouragement from the authorial front lines. John MacFarlane provided excellent legal advice, and Phil Grant accounting advice. Michael Goldberg provided a valuable tax law perspective. Jim Rogers and Morley Goldberg also read the manuscript and provided valuable feedback. *The Facts of Life* is a better book because of their efforts.

I have been privileged to work with and be schooled by some of the best insurance people in Canada: David McEwan, Ray Halpenny, Donald Harding, and the late Paul Leonard. I am deeply indebted to them all.

My co-workers at Industrial Alliance, and more specifically the Ontario office, have helped me get to this point. More importantly, they (especially my assistant, Pat Davies) have put up with me for the last fourteen years. I thank them all.

Many other colleagues have spent time and energy reading and discussing the contents of this book. Stan Cameron, Marc Guay, Fergus Ducharme, Leonard Vis, and Damian Borges all offered their insights at a point when Susan and I were too close to the book to see it clearly anymore.

Susan and I would like to thank our families: Denise, Fraser, and Spencer Grimes, Joyce and Freddy Kingsford, Rae and Perry Dellio, and especially the late John Grimes; Rachel Warburton, and Ruth and Morley Goldberg. Without their love and support, this book would just be one of those great dreams that never came true!

PAUL GRIMES
JANUARY 2002

Introduction

Q: Who wants to read a book on life insurance?
A: More people than you think.

Life insurance.

What comes to mind when you read those two words? If you're like most Canadians, you think of two things, most likely, neither of them pleasant: death and salespeople. Oh, and maybe the fact that life insurance can be about as exciting as watching paint dry. Woody Allen once remarked, "There are worse things than death. I mean, if you've ever spent an evening with an insurance salesman, you know exactly what I mean."

As a result of this mindset, Canadians are in a bit of a quandary: because we think life insurance is boring or depressing, many of us haven't done the work necessary to research and purchase a suitable policy. We're left wondering if we're underinsured or overinsured, if we're paying too much for insurance, or if the policy we have is appropriate for our financial and family situations.

Those of us without insurance wonder if we need it, and if so, how much and where to get it. Can we afford it? Can we afford *not* to have it?

What's more, the life insurance industry, like the rest of the financial marketplace, is evolving at breakneck speed.

Banks, brokerages, mutual fund companies — even credit card companies and grocery stores — are jumping on the life insurance bandwagon. Complicated products like "universal" life insurance are becoming increasingly popular as investors look for ways to minimize taxes while maximizing coverage and returns. You can now purchase life insurance over the Internet. But are you getting good value? Is it safe?

With new players and products flooding the insurance market, Canadian consumers face more choice — and more confusion — than ever before. And more than ever, you need a map to guide you through the increasingly complicated maze of insurance options. When it comes to making decisions about life insurance, you need the advice of someone you can trust.

That's where *The Facts of Life* comes in. Our goal in writing this book was to provide the average (and not-so-average) Canadian with a comprehensive, easy-to-understand guide to life insurance and its related products. No pressure and no salespeople. But that was only part of our challenge. We also wanted to write a book that you'd actually enjoy reading. We figured you wouldn't learn much if you kept falling asleep. And so we created a cast of characters to accompany you on your guided tour through the life insurance maze. Enter the extended Stonehouse clan: you can follow the exploits of the four Stonehouse siblings and their parents, partners, relatives, and friends as their Uncle Charles, a retired industry veteran who knows the insurance business inside and out, teaches them the basics of life insurance. (And Uncle Charles whips up a mean batch of cinnamon buns to boot!)

Studies show that people buy insurance five to seven times over the life course: when they marry or form a significant partnership; when they have a first child and any subsequent children; when they make a major purchase like a house; in their peak earning years; when they retire; and as they begin to wind down their estates and plan their wills. That's why we've organized *The Facts of Life* according to the typical life course of relationships and career. Over a summer vacation at the idyllic family cottage in the Gatineaus, Uncle Charles provides the members of his extended family — including newlyweds just starting a family, a young couple with dependent children, a self-employed writer, an Internet startup owner, about-to-be retirees, and ageing parents with retirements to fund and estates to plan — with the information they need to buy the appropriate type and amount of life insurance. The class-room is the cottage, and the students are Charles's siblings, nieces, and nephews, and their families. Each pupil arrives at the cottage at a different time in the summer; each is looking for some R&R and leaves with unexpected but welcome insurance advice specific to his or her particular stage of life.

A born teacher, Uncle Charles guides his pupils through the basics of life insurance, explains its place within a financial plan, and makes suggestions about the type and quantity of coverage, as well as where to buy insurance products. He'll debunk common myths about life insurance and provide a plethora of tips to make the buying process pain-free.

Charles and his crew don't just stick to life insurance, however. They also discuss what he terms "life insurance for the living": those products designed to protect and enhance quality of life for Canadians and their loved ones — while they're still alive. They look at disability, long-term care, and critical illness insurance, as well as living benefits.

At the back of this book, you'll find simple worksheets for assessing and planning your own life insurance needs and strategies, as well as resources for more information.

This book focuses on the "life" in life insurance — the real-life needs and concerns of Canadians, who don't want to be bored by overly technical manuals or intimidated by salespeople. Our aim was to create a sympathetic cast of characters whose family and financial profiles mirror those of everyday Canadians at all ages and stages of life. We hope that you'll find your own needs mirrored in those of our characters, and that you'll be able to return to *The Facts of Life* again and again as those needs change. We also hope that we've provided a fun, user-friendly tool to give you the knowledge and confidence you need to make the right choices when it comes to life insurance.

1

THE FACTS OF LIFE

EVER have one of those moments in life when you feel as though you're on a movie set? You know what I mean. You're standing on a train platform as the train pulls away carrying the person you love; you say, "I do"; you catch that ball way out in left field to win the game, and your cheering teammates carry you across the field on their shoulders. It's as though a camera crew should be there, with a director yelling, "Cut! That's a wrap."

Well, I was having one of those moments.

Picture it: a small banquet hall filled with fifty or so of my friends and colleagues from work. Champagne corks pop and cameras flash as those friends and colleagues applaud and raise glasses of bubbly. "To Charles Stonehouse, retiring after forty years in the business!" There are speeches, toasts, and roasts; some of my colleagues, the guys who worked with me through the early part of my career, try their best to embarrass me with stories of my days as a rookie. (Sometimes they succeed.) Younger folks, the men and women I'd mentored over the years, make speeches about me as a teacher and a leader, and I blush. I never imagined at the time that I was having that kind of effect on a young person's life, but apparently I was. There's even the proverbial gold watch, engraved with my name and my years with the company. It rests heavy and solid on my wrist, and it feels good.

I had cleaned out my office the day before. Talk about sentimental. I'd stood in my office, the place where I had worked for the past decade, and looked around the now barren room. I had placed the last of my belongings into a cardboard banker's box: plaques commemorating my years of service and awards won; paperweights; and framed pictures of my late wife, my nieces and nephews, and office events. I shook my head fondly as I switched off the light and walked out that door for the last time. I had to admit I would miss the place, the constant hum of activity and the people I'd worked with each day. But it was time to move on.

Welcome to retirement, Charles Stonehouse!

"Cut! That's a wrap!"

◆ ◆ ◆

"Charles!" My regional sales manager, Stan, waved his hand in front of my face. "Earth to Charles! You're in another world."

I laughed. "Sorry, it must be the bubbly. I'm on cloud nine!"

"Well, you're going to float even higher after you see what we've got for you," said Stan. "Come on over to the office table."

"You guys didn't have to get me anything," I protested as I excused myself from the head table and followed Stan. My officemates were waiting for me, grinning, a large wrapped box on the table in front of them.

"It's not what you're expecting, Charles," said Stan. "But we think you'll get a kick out of it."

"You really shouldn't have," I said as I tore off the paper.

The package held something I had never heard of before: a bread-making machine.

"A bread-making machine?" I asked, turning the box over and trying to make out the instructions. "Well . . . wow! It's just what I've always wanted!" I hoped I sounded reasonably convincing. What on earth would I do with this gadget?

"You just put in all the ingredients, wait a few hours, and . . . presto!" chimed in Marcia, my assistant and office manager. "You've got a fresh-baked loaf of bread, ready to go!"

"You sound like an infomercial," I told her. "Do you have shares in the company that makes these things?"

"We figure you've got to develop some new hobbies now that you're retired," said Stan. "So we've given you a head start."

I had no idea how they'd decided on bread making as the key to my retirement happiness, but since I hadn't yet come up with a plan of my own for the rest of my post-work life, I supposed I should be open to suggestions. In fact, I'll admit that I was a little worried about how I'd occupy my time once I wasn't putting in the eight- and nine-hour workdays I was accustomed to.

My worries, however, were outweighed by excitement, even anticipation. It was time for a change, and even though I didn't quite know what that change was, I was looking forward to it. Forty years' worth of work was enough, in my opinion. I'd been in the life insurance business for a long, long time — I had gone from knocking on doors as a salesperson to managing an entire region of agents, and the past few years especially had been both heady and draining. The industry was in a state of flux. Private companies had gone public — now our clients were also shareholders, and we all watched the stock market tables religiously. Banks and mutual fund brokers were now selling insurance; you could even buy it on-line. There was more competition — not, in my opinion, a bad thing — and also more confusion. Some insurance companies had merged; others had been taken over. One big one — Confederation Life — had even collapsed, leaving us all a little shaken about the future of our own jobs.

Industry flux certainly hadn't passed by my office. In fact, it was the main reason I had opted to retire when I had. My own company was merging with another firm; we'd been bought out. I'd been offered a new position in the merged company: branch manager of the insurance section of the company's financial-services centre in Oshawa, Ontario. But I'd been living in Kingston for my entire adult life, and the idea of moving at this stage hadn't appealed to me. The generous early retirement package did, however, and I decided to call it quits. The question was, What next?

The past few years had been tough ones personally as well. Anne and I had been married for thirty-five years when she died of breast cancer. That was five years ago. You don't get over losing your partner in life, I had discovered, but you do learn to get through the immense grief, to reach a place of acceptance, maybe even some kind of understanding or peace. It's a cliché, I know, but Anne and I had been best friends. We hadn't had any children — not that we hadn't wanted to, but it had never happened for us. Instead, we had spent much of our free time together, going to plays and concerts, taking trips, and acting as a set of second parents to our extended family of nieces and nephews. Anne had a way with people. She had been an occupational therapist, and had also taught in the OT program at Queen's University. Her patients, and her students, responded to her warmth and genuine interest in their lives and health.

I had thrown myself into work after Anne's death — another cliché, I now realize. I had healed a lot in the past five years, but the spectre of retirement had brought up some of my old grief, and a couple of worries about how I'd be spending the next years. I'd always thought that Anne and I would spend a long, healthy retirement together. Now

I was on my own. I'd been on a few dates in the past couple of years, all with lovely women, but no one had really stood out for me as "the one." Maybe now I was ready to start a new relationship? A new career? A whole new phase of life?

"This gift is great," I said to my staff. "It's time for this old dog to try a few new tricks. Thanks."

◆ ◆ ◆

I woke up late the next day, a beautiful Saturday morning in early June. I collected the paper from the front porch, put on a pot of coffee, and studied the boxes I had left on the kitchen table the night before. I took the framed pictures from my box of office memorabilia and put them on the mantel and coffee tables. The rest of the stuff, I decided, could go in the basement. No need to hang my Regional Manager of the Year Award on the wall here!

Then, shaking my head, I looked at the bread-maker box. Wasn't making bread something that was supposed to take time and effort? Still, curiosity got the better of me, and I opened the box. Inside, someone — Marcia, I suspected — had placed a small jar of bread-machine yeast, with a note that read, "You'll need this!" The machine itself looked like a cross between a humidifier and a cooler: white, with rounded corners, a computerized control panel on top, and a window that, I presumed, allowed you to see how your loaf was progressing. I picked up the instruction manual and thumbed through it. Instructions, diagrams, warnings . . . recipes. Classic white, carrot, oat bran, oatmeal, rye, cheese and onion, whole wheat, egg bread, pumpkin, cinnamon buns . . . my mouth actually watered. I got out the flour. Maybe Stan, Marcia, and the rest of them were savvier than I had given them credit for.

I decided to start at the beginning, with the old-fashioned white loaf. As I carefully measured the ingredients into the machine, I began to hum. Milk, water, an egg, some butter, the dry ingredients, topped off with precisely one and three-quarters of a teaspoon of active dry yeast. Done. I plugged in the machine and pressed the Start button. For a second, nothing happened. Then the machine clanked loudly to life. Looking through the window, I watched as the lumpy mass of ingredients soon morphed into a ragged ball of dough, which the machine's kneading function quickly whipped into shape. Fascinating. After about ten minutes, the clanking, whirring sounds stopped, and the machine began to let the dough rise.

I sat at the kitchen table, the machine warm beside me, kind of like a pet. Perhaps I'd learn to cook more in my retirement. I could enrol in a cooking class in town. Maybe they had one for single seniors. I could look at community college courses. Learn to dance, perhaps? Travel? Maybe I'd look into doing some renovations on the house, the kinds of things that Anne and I had always talked about, like refinishing the floors or replacing the kitchen cabinets, but that we'd never seemed to find the time for. I could volunteer: I had been canvassing with the Canadian Cancer Society, but perhaps I could step up my efforts there and do more — chair a committee, or sit on a board somewhere? The possibilities for the years ahead seemed endless. A little daunting, but also tremendously exciting. I would need to get used to the idea of having free time for the rest of my life.

Maybe the local community college, or one of the hotels, had cooking courses. I could find out on the Internet. I went upstairs to the den and hooked up my laptop computer. As it booted up, I glanced around the room. The walls could use a fresh coat of paint, I decided. Another thing to add to my retirement list.

Before getting on-line, I checked my e-mail. Three new messages: two from life insurance discussion groups, and one from my brother, Peter. I glanced at the two industry messages — nothing new there — and then opened Peter's message.

From: Peter Stonehouse <pstonehouse@mailbox.com>
To: Charles Stonehouse <cstonehouse@lifeins.com>
Date: June 16, 2001 9:54 AM
Subject: Come on up to visit!

Charles,

So this is the big week, isn't it? Retired after
how many years? Must be nearly 40, I think, of service.
Quite a change.

Catherine and I were talking about you this morning,
and came up with an idea that we hope you'll think
is a great one. If you don't have summer plans yet,
why not come up to the cottage with us? We opened up
the place about two weeks ago, and it's beautiful as
usual. There's lots of room, we'd love to see you, and
you can stay as long as you'd like, a few weeks or the
whole summer if you want. We don't come home until
after Labour Day.

At the very least, you know we expect to see you at
the annual Labour Day party!

Give it some thought.

Catherine sends her love and can't wait to see you.

Peter

Kismet. Karma. Serendipity. Synchronicity. Fate. Whatever
you wanted to call it, Peter, in the role of wiser older brother,
had read my mind.

Perhaps it wasn't as much of a coincidence as it seemed.
I'd had quite a few discussions with Peter and his wife,
Catherine, over the past couple of years about retirement
and other transitions. They, my sister, Joyce, and her husband, and my nieces and nephews had provided the support
and encouragement I'd needed during Anne's illness and

after her death. And this invitation was an extension of that support as I made another transition.

Peter and Catherine owned a beautiful cottage in the Gatineau Hills, outside of Ottawa. Ever since Peter had retired, they'd spent most of every summer up there. The place had been in Catherine's family for at least a couple of generations, and I'd spent many a long weekend there, with Anne and on my own, enjoying the lake and the surroundings, as well as the company of my family. I'd watched my nieces and nephews — Peter and Catherine's four children, and Joyce and Rob's two — grow up there. More recently, their children — my great-nieces and -nephews — had continued the cycle.

What better place to ease into retirement? I could go up to the cottage for a few weeks, stay longer if I felt like it or come back home if I got restless. Any community college courses wouldn't start until September. And I'd be surrounded by family.

On the other hand . . . I'd be surrounded by family. Would we get along? Would we get bored with one another? How would I keep myself occupied there? What if —

The phone rang, cutting short my worrying. It was Marcia.

"Hi, Charles," she said. "Just thought I'd call and see how you were doing. It was a great party last night!"

I had worked closely with Marcia for nearly ten years — since I'd started my job as regional manager for our company's Eastern Ontario office. She was one of those eminently capable people: she knew where every file was and kept the place running like clockwork. No wonder she'd been offered the position of office manager in Oshawa, in the merged company's much larger and busier office. She had accepted, and I knew she'd do a wonderful job.

But Marcia's talents extended beyond simply managing the office. She had a sixth sense about people. If you were sick, worried about something, or just having a bad day,

Marcia knew and did her best to let you know that she cared, even with just a few friendly words. She was as important a member of my team as any sales agent. And so I wasn't surprised now that she was calling. I think she'd picked up on my anxieties about retirement, and she would want to make sure that I was doing okay.

"I'm good," I told her. "Really. And thanks for the bread-maker. Would you believe I've got a loaf baking in it right now?"

She laughed. "I knew you'd like that thing."

I told Marcia about Peter and Catherine's invitation. If I'd had any doubts about going to the Gatineau Hills, she quickly erased them.

"That's a wonderful idea!" she said. "You've been telling me for months that you need a change of scenery, some-where to recharge your batteries."

I had? Yes, she was right. I had.

"And you've been talking about how you wish you could spend more time with your family."

She was right again. I'd wanted to see more of everyone, especially since my nieces and nephews had spread out across the country. Lindsay and Daniel were in Ottawa; Karin was in Vancouver; Andrew and Rebecca and their kids were in Montreal; and Lisa, Spencer, and Fraser were in Toronto. I was sure they'd all be up at the cottage during various summer weekends. It would be a chance to spend some relaxed, uninterrupted time with them. The invitation was sounding better and better.

"Thanks, Marcia," I told her. "You just helped me make my decision."

We chatted for a few more minutes, and Marcia extracted from me a promise that I'd take care of myself and have a great time at the cottage. I thanked her for everything, and wished her the best of luck in her new job.

We hung up. I reread Peter's message and hit Reply.

From: Charles Stonehouse <cstonehouse@lifeins.com>
To: Peter Stonehouse <pstonehouse@mailbox.com>
Date: June 16, 2001 12:37 PM
Subject: RE: Come on up to visit!

Peter,

Thanks to you and Catherine for the invitation.
Sounds like a great idea, and exactly what I need
right now. I'll call to discuss details.

Retirement so far (less than twenty-four hours)
keeps getting better and better. I'm learning how
to make bread!

Chas

I hit Send. Then I fiddled around for a while on the
Internet, researching some community college programs
and volunteer opportunities with the cancer society, and
checking out a do-it-yourself home-renovation site.

I must have been on-line a couple of hours when my
thoughts were interrupted by a pinging sound. I started,
trying to figure out where it was coming from. The phone?
No. Then I realized: the bread machine! I entered the kitchen,
where the smell of freshly baked bread hung in the air.
I opened the top and removed a perfect, golden brown loaf
of classic white from the pan. It was barely cool before I cut
the first slice, spread it with butter, and took a bite.

Delicious.

RECIPES FOR SUCCESS

1 In 1999, several of Canada's largest life and health insurers began the process of "demutualization," or going public and trading on the stock market. As a result, eligible policyholders were transformed into shareholders of publicly traded companies.

2 The past few years have also seen an explosion of life insurance products and vendors, and increased competition, which has left consumers with more choice — and more confusion. More than ever, Canadian consumers need a reliable guide to lead them through the process of buying insurance.

3 Canadian retirees are younger than ever! In 1995, the median retirement age in Canada was sixty-two, down from sixty-five in 1973. According to Statistics Canada, retiring Canadians can expect to live, on average, thirteen years in good health, free of work obligations and pursuing personal goals. Good financial and personal planning can contribute to an enjoyable retirement.

4 Even old dogs can learn new tricks!

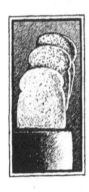

2

MAPMAKER, MAPMAKER, MAKE ME A MAP:

THE ROAD TO SOUND FINANCIAL PLANNING

THE next couple of weeks were taken up with preparations for my trip to the Gatineau Hills. My next-door neighbour kindly agreed to water the plants, collect and forward the mail, and keep an eye on the house. I cancelled the newspaper, hired someone to take care of mowing the lawn and tending the garden, and for good measure, installed motion lights at the front and back doors and over the garage. Another one of those things I had planned to do for far too long but hadn't got around to. Retirement had its perks.

I bought a couple of new pairs of shorts and a bathing suit, some gifts for Peter and Catherine, and a few good, thick novels. I was going to catch up on my reading, especially all those books I'd wanted to read my whole life but hadn't got around to, like *War and Peace*, *The Brothers Karamazov*, and *The Invisible Man*. Got the car tuned up and the fluid levels checked. Peter, however, had taken care of the route planning. Despite my protests that I had been there dozens of times in the past, he just had to show me one of his latest software tricks. When he sent me road maps via e-mail, I had to laugh.

My brother's always been something of a technology nut

— what the marketing people call an early adaptor. He went to the Royal Military College in Kingston after high school and got a degree in electrical engineering. If they had offered computer engineering back then, I'm sure he would have taken it. After a few years of military service, he started working for IBM, while doing an M.B.A. at night school. He finally took an early retirement package from IBM in 1990, and he's dabbled in some business-development and technology consulting ever since.

Mostly, though, I think he's having fun playing with all the new computer programs that keep coming on the market. You can take the guy out of IBM, I suppose, but you can't take IBM out of the guy. Actually, I credit Peter with keeping me up to date on the latest technology; because of his influence, I was one of the first people in my office to have a laptop computer, and I made sure my sales agents had them, too, so they would be able to give presentations to clients in their homes and have complex financial information at their fingertips. Now I can't imagine how we ever got by without them.

Every time I see Peter, he's got some new computer toy or program or game to show me. He sends me pictures of the kids and grandkids via e-mail. When his latest grandchild, Jack, was born a few years ago, he took pictures of him with his new digital camera and made a web site of baby photos so that friends and relatives all over the world could see how cute he was.

The latest program he's got hold of is a trip planner. You plug in your starting point and destination, and the computer spits out a full-colour map of the best route to take, complete with itinerary. Now whenever he and Catherine drive anywhere more than a few kilometres away, he maps out the best possible route using the computer. They planned a trip to Florida last winter, and while Catherine spent most of her time packing, he was busy on the computer, finding the best way to get there, right down to how many minutes the entire drive would take. Sometimes I wish life was as easy to plan.

But it isn't. Everything went like clockwork on the way down to the Sunshine State. But on the way home, after two weeks of discount shopping, golf, and early bird dinner specials, Peter and Catherine nearly drove right into the hurricane that was drenching the Carolinas in more than one hundred centimetres of rain. The highways were closed, the roads were a disaster, and a few unfortunate travellers lost their lives in that storm. My brother's map didn't mean a lot as he and Catherine waited out the storm in a nice, dry hotel room, playing travel Scrabble and reading their novels. That's kind of how life goes, I guess. You make your plans and hope for the best, and then pray you have the resources to deal with all the unexpected stuff.

So I laughed when I opened the graphic files attached to his e-mail: two maps to the cottage — one the shorter, more efficient, but ultimately none-too-pretty route along the 401, east to Highway 416; the other the winding, scenic road that went through Smiths Falls.

"Take your pick," he had typed. "Either way, we'll be happy to see you when you get here."

◆ ◆ ◆

Finally, my departure date arrived. I stood outside and looked at the car, my two suitcases in the back, my laptop computer (a security blanket of sorts; I hadn't quite got used to the idea that I was retired), and the bottles of wine and the fruit basket I had purchased as gifts for my brother and his wife. Did I have everything I needed?

No, I realized. One thing was missing. I went back inside and returned about ten minutes later. Under one arm, I carried a bag that contained flour (white and whole wheat — I had branched out), yeast, raisins, cinnamon, and various other dry goods. Under the other arm, I held the bread-maker. If I was going to be an extended houseguest, I reasoned, I could at least make myself useful. I'd provide the daily bread.

In retrospect, I would realize that I'd provided a lot more to my extended family that summer. And they, in turn, would take my life in an entirely new direction. But I didn't know that at the beginning of my journey.

◆ ◆ ◆

I had decided upon the scenic route. It seemed appropriate, now that I was retired, to take the road less travelled — the whole "focus on the journey as well as the destination" philosophy I was trying to cultivate.

I popped a CD into the player as I pulled onto the highway. With the music — the recent Beatles *One* album — playing, I hit the open road.

Peter's map lay on the front seat next to me. It was funny, I thought, but in a way, I'd been making maps for people for much of my career. Life insurance, I firmly believed, was about planning, about figuring out how to get from here to there. When I created life insurance plans for my clients, I'd often ask them where they wanted to be in ten, twenty, thirty years. And how were they going to get there? Not surprisingly, most people wanted pretty much the same things: to work at a job they enjoyed, educate their children, retire in good health and spend time with their families, and see their children grow up, be successful, and start families of their own. With some minor variations, I would say that the vast majority of my clients fit into this mould. My job, I figured, was a cross between cartographer and travel agent: I created the map that got them from here to there, and advised them about the various ways they could navigate that journey.

And if an unexpected obstacle — like a premature death, illness, or disability — fell like a tree across the road from here to there, life insurance was the detour, the alternative route to those goals. In the same way that Peter had for me, I had created a few different plans, or road maps, for my clients, showing them the various ways they could achieve their financial goals and personal desires. Life insurance was an important part of these road maps, the Plan B that I hoped none of my clients would ever have to use, but which, I knew from experience, many of them would.

If being in the insurance industry for four decades had taught me anything, it was that plans don't always work out the way you expect them to. I had seen families devastated by unexpected losses. I had tried to teach my clients to always have a backup plan, and I thought I had taken my own advice.

But as far as my personal life went, I was starting to realize that I hadn't done such a great job of thinking about good old Plan B. Here I was, the guy who made plans for everyone else. I had thought that Anne and I would grow old together, like Peter and Catherine, but that hadn't happened. And although I had profited from my own careful financial planning, I hadn't given much thought to what it might be like to spend the next twenty years on my own.

Maybe, I thought, this summer would be a good time to start thinking about my own personal Plan B, also known as the Rest of My Life.

◆ ◆ ◆

About three and a half hours later, I pulled onto the winding dirt road that led in to the cottage from the highway. As I stopped the car, I tooted the horn. Moments later, the front door opened and my brother stepped out into the grassy clearing in front of the building.

"Charles!" he said, coming towards me and clapping me on the back. "Welcome! Catherine's reading on the dock. I was just checking my e-mail."

"Of course you were," I said, laughing. "You've got the beautiful outdoors to enjoy, so of course you're on-line."

"I got an e-mail from Lindsay and Daniel," he continued, choosing to ignore my sarcasm. "They're planning on arriving in time for dinner. So we'll have a full house."

"Lindsay and Daniel are coming? That's great!"

"Oh, yes," said my sister-in-law, who had emerged, sunhat on head, from around the side of the house. "They've both got the summer off, and they plan on spending a few weeks up here before they have to go back to the city and prepare for the baby's arrival. In fact, all the kids will be here over the course of the summer. We sent out an open invitation, and they've all made plans to get up here, even if it's just for a long weekend here and there. It's wonderful to see you, Charles," she added, giving me a hug. "We were so glad when you said you would come."

"I'm glad to be here, too. And I can't wait to see the kids."

Lindsay is Peter and Catherine's youngest child, and Daniel is her husband. They're expecting their first child sometime in September. (When they announced the pregnancy, Peter's e-mail message heading had read, "My baby's having a baby!") I could hardly believe that my mischievous niece would soon be a mom. I've always had a special place in my heart for her; she's an impetuous, generous person, and we take great delight in teasing each other. She'd found a wonderful match in Daniel. He's more reserved than she is, but they complement each other. And now I'd get to spend some extended time with them.

"Let me help you with your bags," said Peter as he moved towards the car. "We thought we'd put you in the guest house, so you'd be close by but have a little privacy as well." He grabbed one of my suitcases and reached for the bread-maker. "What's this?"

"That," I said, "should go in the kitchen. It's a retirement present from my office, and I'm having a lot of fun with it."

I explained the bread-maker's workings to Peter and Catherine, and promised that I'd make dinner rolls for them that evening.

◆ ◆ ◆

"These are fabulous, Uncle Charles!" Lindsay was in the middle of devouring her second roll. "I could eat a million of these."

Daniel rolled his eyes. "She hasn't stopped eating for the past six months," he said, "and you can hardly tell she's due to give birth in another three."

Daniel was right. My niece looked great: healthy, happy — dare I say glowing? Or is it out of fashion to say that pregnant women glow? And despite her appetite, she didn't seem to have added a lot of weight to her athletic frame. I guessed it was a perk of being a physical-education teacher. Daniel taught English and history at the same high school in Ottawa. They both had a way with kids, and I had no doubt that they'd be great parents.

We were nearly done dinner. Peter had thrown a salmon on the barbecue, and Catherine had made a huge salad. With rolls and one of the bottles of wine I'd brought up, it was a perfect, early summer cottage feast. We ate outside on the deck, listening to the sounds of the lake. It was almost completely dark by the time the meal was over, and I remembered how much brighter the stars were up here than in Kingston. How could I have questioned my decision to spend the summer in the Gatineau Hills?

"How much time are you taking for maternity leave?" I asked my niece.

"A year," Lindsay answered. "I'm taking advantage of the new employment insurance rules. It'll be less money, but I really think I'll want to be at home with the baby for as long as possible. At least, that's what I'm saying now. I could always go back in time for the second semester if I need to."

"And I assume you've got life insurance covered, as well as unemployment?"

"Life insurance?" Lindsay looked at me blankly. "We've got some coverage at work."

"Are you sure it's enough?" I asked "I doubt it is."

"Uncle Charles," said my niece with a laugh, "are you trying to sell me insurance? I thought you'd retired."

"I've still got the job of concerned uncle," I countered. "I'm not trying to sell you life insurance, but I do think that with a baby coming, you'll probably need a lot more coverage than what your benefit plan provides."

"I don't know," mused Daniel. "I guess we haven't thought that much about it."

"You should," I replied. "It's important."

"I'm sure you're right, Uncle Charles," said Lindsay. "I don't know if we have enough insurance — I have no idea how much is enough. But" — and here she pouted winningly — "we're on vacation. The last thing I feel like talking about is life insurance and dying."

I got the message. And I was beginning to realize just what retirement meant. I would have to stop seeing the world only through the eyes of an insurance professional. On the other hand, this was my niece — and my soon-to-be great-niece or -nephew. I had spent a lot of time thinking about Plan B today. Didn't they owe it to themselves to make sure they had their own Plan B?

"Okay, okay," I told Lindsay and Daniel. "I'll lay off you guys, at least for a little while. I just want to say one thing, and then I'll keep my mouth shut."

"What?" they asked in unison.

"You mentioned that you didn't know if you had enough life insurance. Well, I'll tell you something: no one *ever* has enough life insurance. No one. Ever."

They looked at me blankly. Finally, Lindsay spoke up.

"No one ever has enough life insurance? What do you mean?"

Peter and Catherine both smiled to themselves as they listened to my answer.

"I'm not going to tell you what I mean. You and Daniel think about it; you'll figure it out."

I got up from the table. "You know, everyone, it's been a long, exciting day for me. I think I'm ready to turn in. Goodnight."

RECIPES FOR SUCCESS

1   The successful financial and insurance plan takes into account both short- and long-term goals. Where do you want to be in five years? In twenty-five years? How will you get there? Life insurance is one of the cornerstones of any sound financial plan.

2   Life never works out exactly as planned — never underestimate the importance of a Plan B. Often, life insurance plays an important role when plans don't play out as expected.

3   Getting hitched? Moving in together? Having a baby? Starting a business? If you answered yes to any of those questions, it might be time to start thinking about purchasing life insurance. If your premature death would cause financial hardship to a family member, employee, or colleague, you should consider life insurance.

3

LIFE GOES ON:

LIFE INSURANCE 101

I woke up early the next morning and wandered into the kitchen just in time to catch the gentle ping-ping-ping of the bread-maker letting me know that my dough was ready. The evening before, I'd put in the ingredients for cinnamon-raisin rolls and set the timer. The machine began working its magic process of kneading and rising while I slept, and when I opened the top at 6:30 a.m., a glob of just-risen dough was ready.

I love working in the kitchen — doing almost any work, in fact — in the early hours of the morning, when everyone else is still asleep and the day is young. I get my best thinking done at these times. And I was happy to be alone with my thoughts as I shaped the dough into a rectangle; slathered it with butter (what the hell, I was on holidays), sugar, cinnamon, and raisins; and rolled it into a long cylinder. Whistling softly, I cut the dough crosswise into twelve pieces and placed them on a cookie sheet, covered, to rise again. My task completed, I went outside on the deck to be by myself for a little while longer, surrounded by nature and my thoughts.

It was going to be a gorgeous day. The sun was up over a

lake that resembled a mirror, its surface not yet disturbed by swimmers, canoeists, and boaters. The only sounds were the lazy lapping of water against the dock and the twittering of birds in the trees surrounding me. Oh, and the very occasional hum of a mosquito. In this idyllic setting, I began to think that I had made the right decision to spend the summer here, among loved ones. It would be great to see my brother and his wife, and to spend time with my nieces and nephews and their young families.

I frowned, however, as I thought about the previous night's conversation. I wasn't happy to hear that one of my favourite nieces hadn't given much thought to financial planning. But I was even unhappier with myself for forcing the issue. You're on holiday, I reminded myself. In fact, you're retired. You don't need to fret about the life insurance needs of others any more. And you *definitely* don't need to be offering unsolicited advice to your relatives. That would wear out your welcome faster than anything else.

But I couldn't help thinking about Lindsay's rather cavalier attitude towards life insurance and financial planning in general. Especially with a baby on the way, and her and Daniel's plans to buy a house . . . but I was doing it again! Okay, you meddling old man, I told myself, only half-jokingly, here's the deal: no unsolicited advice. Gone are the days of knocking on people's doors to ask them if they'd like to buy insurance. If anyone asks you your opinion, you can give it. Otherwise, keep it zipped.

On that note, I fetched my copy of *War and Peace* and opened it. A couple dozen pages or so later, I looked up from the novel and at my watch. The cinnamon buns would be ready to bake by now, I figured. I went back inside the cottage to check. They had risen nicely and doubled in size. They'd need only about twenty minutes to bake. I put them in the oven, and put on a pot of coffee.

Ten minutes later, the kitchen was filled with delicious

smells — cinnamon, baking bread, and the rich scent of Colombian dark roast. I knew I wouldn't be alone much longer.

And I was right. As I was taking the cinnamon rolls, now golden brown, out of the oven, Lindsay wandered into the kitchen, rubbing her eyes.

"It smells like heaven in here," she said. "What on earth are you making?"

I broke off a sticky bun and put it on a plate. "Here," I said. "Be careful — it's hot."

Lindsay looked at me and grinned. "This is great. I'm so famished these days, I bet I could eat all of those by myself."

"Well, you *are* eating for two," I said.

"Some days I feel like I'm eating for three or four," she retorted. "It's dangerous. Could you please pour me a cup of coffee, Uncle Charles? I've cut back, I swear, but I still need that first cup in the morning."

"Everything in moderation," I replied as I poured two steaming mugs. We moved out on to the deck, but not before Lindsay put another cinnamon roll on her plate. I pretended not to notice. Moderation is subjective.

Outside, the lake was no longer flat, as swimmers and boaters had begun to stir. We settled into deck chairs and sipped our coffee.

"You know, Uncle Charles, I'm sorry if I was a bit flip at dinner last night. I actually thought a lot about what you said, about nobody ever having enough insurance. Daniel and I talked about it before we went to bed. And I think I know what you meant."

"And what did I mean?"

"Well" — Lindsay stretched her legs out on the deck chair — "if I had a choice between Daniel and millions of dollars, I'd still pick Daniel. At least, most days." She smiled wickedly. "And the same goes for this one in here." She stroked her rounded belly. "I mean, I know that if anything happened to this baby, you could offer me truckloads of money, but it wouldn't make me feel any better. And if something happened to me, all the money in the world couldn't bring this baby back its mother, or me to Daniel."

I nodded.

"So I think what you meant is that no amount of life insurance can ever *replace* the people you love — but it can make it financially easier for the people they leave behind."

"Well put," I said.

"Soooo," she continued, "you've got me thinking that maybe I should know a little more about all this stuff than I do right now, what with the baby and us thinking about buying a house, and all that. I don't really like thinking about money all that much, or about the possibility of death, but I guess it's time to grow up and learn."

"Well," I said, trying to hide my relief, "I can give you the names of a few agents — good ones — to talk to."

"But why would I want to talk to an agent when I've got you?" asked Lindsay. "We — Daniel and I — were actually hoping that you might be able to give us some tips. I think we'd feel intimidated by an agent."

We looked up at the sound of the door opening. Daniel emerged onto the porch, wearing a pair of sweat shorts and an old T-shirt. He carried a mug of coffee in one hand and the remains of a cinnamon roll in the other.

"These are great!" he said, his mouth full. "Did you make them, Charles?"

"Believe it or not, I did," I replied. "Or at least, the bread-maker did, with just a bit of help from me."

"Can you give me the bread-maker's telephone number?" he asked, ruffling Lindsay's hair. She swatted his hand, then opened her mouth. He popped the last bit of his cinnamon roll into it.

"Daniel," she said, swallowing, "Uncle Charles is going to teach us about life insurance."

"Good," he said. "We've got a lot to learn."

"Are you sure I'm the one to teach it to you?" I asked. "I mean, I'd be happy to, but you *are* on holiday."

"We're on holiday for eight weeks, Uncle Charles," Lindsay pointed out. "We're teachers. I'm sure we can take some time to learn something from you in there. And better now than when we're busy and exhausted with a new baby."

"Very true," I conceded. "Daniel, you feel the same way?"

"Why not?" he shrugged his shoulders. "No time like the present."

"Well, all right, then," I said. "Welcome to Uncle Charles's Life Insurance Seminars, otherwise known as Life Insurance 101. Refreshments are provided. Of course, you've got the family discount."

Lindsay threw her balled-up napkin at me.

"Okay, I'll stop horsing around," I said. "I'm glad you're taking an interest in financial planning, and I hope I can help out. At the very least, I'd like to make sure you have the knowledge you need to make well-informed decisions. If you know what you need, and want, in terms of life insurance coverage, Lindsay, you won't have a reason to be intimidated or suspicious of the people who sell it to you. You know the saying 'An educated consumer is a good consumer.'"

"Okay, Uncle Charles," she said, laughing. "You've sold me. Educate me!"

"All right," I replied, "let's begin. Let me ask you a question: How much life insurance do you think I own?"

"I don't know," said Lindsay. "You're older — no offence, Uncle Charles . . ."

"None taken," I assured her, smiling.

"And you've got a nice house, and I would bet a lot of investments and savings. Plus you've been selling the stuff for years. I guess you'd have quite a lot of life insurance by now, but I wouldn't know the exact dollar amount. A few hundred thousand bucks? Half a million?"

"You're a little bit off," I told her. "Try zero."

"Zero?" Surprise registered on the faces of my niece and nephew-in-law. "You mean you have no life insurance at all?"

"Well, actually, that's not quite true," I said. "I have a policy I've donated to charity. But for the purposes of this discussion, let's leave that policy out of things. Unlike you, I don't need life insurance."

"Okay, now I'm really confused," said Lindsay. "I thought life insurance was one of those things everybody needed."

"Not at all," I assured her, "although back when I used to sell the stuff, I certainly *did* think that everyone should have life insurance."

"Well, who *does* need it then?" asked Daniel, obviously intrigued.

"Let's answer that question by taking a step back, to the definition of life insurance," I suggested. "What is it?"

The simple question, however, elicited only silence from my usually talkative niece and nephew-in-law. Finally, Daniel spoke up.

"Well, it's a way of making sure that if you die, your family will have enough money to survive without you."

"That's a good start," I said. "But let's define it at the bare-bones level. I would say that life insurance is a contract between you and an insurance company that guarantees that in exchange for the costs, or premiums, you pay, the company will pay tax-free cash — what's known as the death benefit — to your beneficiaries upon your death. Your beneficiary, by the way, is the person or people you've designated to receive the death benefit. Does that make sense?"

They nodded.

"So life insurance, at its simplest, is an agreement between you and a company. You pay them, and in return, they pay your beneficiaries if you die while the policy's in force. And the money they pay is not only tax-free, but also creditor-proof. So even if you've got thousands of dollars in credit card debt, the card company can't claim a share of your death benefit from your beneficiaries. Death benefits also bypass probate, which is the legal process of validating a will."

"What's the advantage in that?" asked Daniel.

"Well, first of all, it means that you don't pay probate fees on the death benefit. Second, it means that if a person's will is contested by his or her heirs, the death benefit isn't part of that contest. A person's estate can be held up for years while people fight over who gets what, but life insurance proceeds can still be paid out immediately to the beneficiaries.

"But perhaps a more important question to address is why people should buy life insurance. Daniel, let's look at what you said about life insurance being a way to ensure that your family has enough money to survive in case you die. What did you mean by that?"

"I guess I meant that if you die, you want to make sure that your family won't fall on hard times, that they'll be able to maintain the same standard of living as they had before you died."

"You've hit the nail on the head! Keep those three words — standard of living — foremost in mind. If you die and there are people who are dependent upon you — or more specifically, your income — to maintain a certain standard of living, then life insurance is one good way of ensuring that your income will be replaced."

"So if you owned a house, you wouldn't have to sell it just to get by," suggested Lindsay.

"Or if you had children in private schools, you wouldn't have to take them out of those schools," added Daniel.

"Exactly. The loss of a loved one is distressing enough without the added stresses of moving, changing schools, or discovering that you can no longer afford the luxuries — or the necessities — that you could before that person died.

And I think it's fair to say that most of us wouldn't want our families to be thrown on hard times if we died prematurely."

"Jeez," said Lindsay, "this is kind of depressing. They should have called it death insurance."

"Actually, you're right," I admitted. "They should have. But really, given how hard it is to make people want to talk about life insurance — let alone buy it — can you imagine how few people would be interested in talking about death insurance? Calling it life insurance seems like a good marketing decision to me."

They laughed.

"I think the most cheerful way to look at it is like this: after your death, life goes on for your loved ones. By having the proper type and amount of insurance, you can make sure that their lives go on without a drop in their standards of living. Maybe a more accurate name would be income-replacement insurance, or standard-of-living insurance."

"Makes sense to me," said Lindsay.

"Which leads us back to the question of who needs it," I said. "Take me. Lindsay, when you said that you thought I'd have a lot of insurance because I have a lot of assets, you made the classic mistake of assuming that life insurance, like property insurance or automobile insurance, is all about what you *have*. Actually, it's got much more to do with *the people you leave behind* and their needs. Ironically, it's usually the people just starting out, with young families, entry-level jobs, and not many assets, who have the greatest need for life insurance. Unfortunately, they're usually the ones who can least afford the premiums. While you'd all be very sad to see me go, I hope, my death wouldn't cause anyone any financial hardship. I have no dependants. I'm a widower, and unlike you in a couple of months, I have no children to support. Further, I'm not in debt, and my savings and assets would be enough to cover my funeral expenses and pay my taxes and any other costs associated with my death. There should even be some left over to leave to favourite nieces and nephews," I added, winking.

"Thanks, Uncle Charles," said Lindsay. "I'm not sure I wanted to hear that, but thanks."

"You're welcome," I said. "I'm not trying to be morbid. The point I *am* trying to make is that life insurance is a great product to own, but only if you need it. You wouldn't buy automobile insurance if you didn't have a car, would you? Similarly, you wouldn't buy a life insurance policy if you didn't have any dependants who would need the death benefits."

"So people with children or spouses to support need life insurance," reiterated Daniel.

"Yes," I said, "unless they have enough in the way of assets and investments that their dependants could get by nicely without the money provided by insurance. If you already have a five-million-dollar trust fund, you probably don't need to buy life insurance because you're self-insured, so to speak. But for most young couples, that's not the case."

"That's certainly not the case for us," said Lindsay. "I mean, we're not lacking for anything, but we've both got student loans and not a lot of savings, aside from the money we're scrounging together to put towards a down payment on a house."

"So with a dependant baby on the way, and no other way of replacing the income lost if one or both of us were to die prematurely, Lindsay and I need life insurance," concluded Daniel.

"Precisely," I confirmed. "And very well put."

"Okay, Uncle Charles," said Lindsay, "I see the need for life insurance, but how much life insurance do I need? How do you figure that out?"

"There are two ways to figure out how much insurance you need," I replied. "Some people recommend an easy rule of thumb: multiply your current income — that is, your gross income, before taxes — by between five and seven.

That'll give you a ballpark figure for how much you need. So going by the rule of thumb, if you earn $35,000 a year as a teacher, you'll probably be looking for coverage in the range of $175,000 to $245,000."

"So the money lasts only for between five and seven years?" asked Daniel.

"No. You don't touch that money, at least not for a very long time. It's what we call capital. The goal is to invest that lump sum of capital and live off the investment earnings or interest it generates — after you've paid off any outstanding debts and other immediate expenses. Many people would invest the death benefit very conservatively and earn interest on the invested capital — as opposed to, say, investing in riskier stocks."

"What rate of return would we need?" asked Lindsay.

"Well, you should always estimate a conservative rate to avoid finding yourself with less money than you need — you know, plan for the worst, hope for the best. I would assume a 6 percent rate of return, on average."

"What's 6 percent of $245,000?" asked Lindsay.

"It's just under $15,000 a year," I said.

"But that won't replace my salary," she said.

"No, it won't," I replied. "Depending on your beneficiaries' needs, seven times your salary may or may not be enough. That's why I'd suggest that you do a detailed needs analysis to determine the appropriate amount of coverage."

"Okay," countered Daniel. "What goes into a needs analysis?"

"Why don't we grab a pen and paper and write down some of these numbers?" I suggested. Daniel jumped up and disappeared into the cottage. Moments later, he returned, armed with writing materials.

"I wish I had a calculator," he said, "but it never occurred to me to bring one to the cottage."

"We should be okay without one for now," I said, smiling.

"In any case, I have my laptop computer with me if it comes to that — old habits die hard."

Lindsay and Daniel looked at me expectantly, Daniel with the pen poised to write.

"You guys are eager!" I remarked. "Okay, let's talk about what sorts of things your insurance benefits will need to cover. There are quite a few factors you'll want to consider.

"First off, you need to figure out how much your survivors will need in annual income to maintain their standard of living, and how much money will come in after your death. You need to think about how much money you'd need to get by each year if you were on your own with a child to raise. Assume, for a moment, that all your debts are paid off."

"On my own, I'd be just fine on my salary," said Daniel.

"Me too," chimed in Lindsay. "But with a baby, it would be different. I'm already planning on taking maternity leave for a year. And I'd like the option of taking longer if I want to, though I do want to go back to work. So I'd need daycare or a nanny. And I'd have to pay for everything myself — like rent, the phone, and utilities. Plus food and clothing, trans-portation . . . I don't know — $50,000 seems about right."

"Same here," Daniel said. "If I were suddenly a single father, I'd probably take a bit of time off work to adjust, and then I'd have to pay for child care. I'll say $50,000 too."

"So if the surviving spouse needs $50,000 a year, before taxes, to get by, and he or she is earning only $35,000 — which is about what I assume younger teachers like you are earning these days —"

"You're right," confirmed Lindsay.

"— then you need to make up a $15,000 annual shortfall. Now, you might make up some of that through income from investments, retirement savings, pensions, and any other sources of income you have. For example, you probably didn't know that you already have two life insurance policies."

"Really?" asked Daniel. "From where?"

"The first one is in the form of government death bene-fits," I replied. "Depending on the number of years you've paid into the Canada Pension Plan, or CPP, and how much you've paid, CPP will pay survivor benefits to your spouse or common-law spouse. It will also pay children's benefits — what some people call orphan benefits — to your children, even if they have one parent remaining and aren't techni-cally orphans. The amounts paid out will vary, and if you've been contributing to CPP for only a few years, they will be lower. But generally, the surviving spouse, if he or she has dependent children, could expect to receive around $400 a month in benefits. Children under the age of eighteen, or under the age of twenty-five and in school, could each expect to receive about $175 monthly. In some provinces, orphan benefits are held in trust by the Attorney General or other government office, and the surviving parent or guardian applies for benefits as they're needed.

"CPP also pays a lump-sum death benefit to the surviving spouse," I continued. "The maximum amount of that ben-efit was decreased to $2,500 in 1998. Of course, these amounts are all subject to change. But it's worth factoring them into your monthly expenses. A monthly payment of $400 in survivor benefits works out to $4,800 a year — that's nearly a third of your $15,000 shortfall right there! Add on orphan benefits, and you've got nearly another $2,000 annually. So your annual shortfall is more like $10,000, give or take a few thousand depending on how long you've been paying CPP."

"There was a guy in my dorm in college who paid for his tuition from orphan benefits," remarked Daniel. "I guess that money can really add up over the years."

"It can," I said, "and many people don't know about it. But it's already made a big dent in the amount of extra money you'll need each year to get by."

"How do you find out how much you're entitled to?" asked Lindsay.

"You'd have to contact Human Resources Development Canada. The amount depends on a bunch of things: how much and how long the deceased paid into the Canada Pension Plan, how old his or her partner is, if they're receiving a pension. Human Resources Development Canada has a web site, and you can also phone them to find out more about your pension and benefits.

"Now that we've established that you'd each need another $10,000 in income each year," I continued, "you need to factor into your life insurance needs a lump sum of capital that, when invested conservatively, would yield that amount in interest each year. Do you follow me?"

They both nodded.

"Assuming an interest rate of 6 percent," I continued, "you'd need a lump sum of about $165,000 to generate that extra $10,000 every year."

Daniel let out a low whistle as he wrote down the number. I wasn't sure if it was for the amount of money or because of my lightning-quick math skills. Undeterred, I continued.

"Second, you generally want to pay off all outstanding debts, like a mortgage, a car loan, student loans, credit card bills, and anything else. Again, losing a loved one is hard enough without trying to manage a debt load on your own. As well, having the mortgage and all other debts paid off is one excellent way of ensuring that your beneficiaries will be able to maintain their standard of living. So when the two of you buy a house, you should also buy enough insurance coverage to pay off the mortgage and any other loans that you have. In any case, banks often require mortgage insurance as a condition of lending you the money. And that's wise — they want to protect the investment they've made in you."

"But what if we're still renting by then?" asked Lindsay.

"You could do a couple of things," I said. "When you calculate how much you need to get by every year, make sure that you include your rental and housing costs in that amount. Or you might consider budgeting enough in insurance to either buy a house outright or provide for a down payment on the type of house you'd like to buy, plus enough capital to generate the mortgage payments each month.

"In your case," I continued, "you're planning on buying a house in the next little while. So let's assume, for the sake of argument, that you've already bought it. What price range are you looking in?"

"Well, you can get a decent little house just outside of Ottawa, in Aylmer, for around $150,000," said Lindsay. "We're hoping to have about $15,000 to put down."

"Have you calculated the other costs of buying a house, like legal fees, property taxes, and land-transfer taxes?"

"Yes," said my niece proudly. "Friends of ours just bought a place and gave us the lowdown on all the costs we hadn't thought about. So we're prepared to spend an extra few thousand once we've found something, plus property taxes every year."

"Good for you," I answered. "Too many first-time homebuyers go into the purchase absolutely unaware of all the extra costs involved. Based on your estimate, let's assume you buy a house for $150,000. You'll have a mortgage of $135,000 to pay after your down payment. That's how much you need to be insured for."

Daniel added the figure to the list.

"And then there are those property taxes," I said. "Where do they go?"

"Oh," said Daniel. "I guess they'd be part of our annual expenses. So we'd need to add another couple thousand dollars to our annual shortfall."

Lindsay nodded.

Daniel crossed out the $10,000 figure and wrote down $12,000 in its place.

"How much are your student loans?" I inquired.

"Mine is at about $9,000," said Daniel, "and Lindsay's is smaller, about $5,000."

"So you'd each need additional insurance in the amount of your student loans."

Daniel made two columns and added the amounts under each of their names.

"Any other debts?"

"Not too much. We're pretty good about credit cards, and the car is Daniel's parents' old clunker, so we don't owe anything on that. We will need to buy a new car in a couple of years, when this one dies — whoops, no pun intended."

"That brings us to the next area of needs planning," I said. "You need to cover all immediate and future lump-sum expenses. Immediate expenses might include all the costs associated with illness and death: your funeral, income taxes after death, any medical bills or legal fees, probate fees for your will, and a period of adjustment when your beneficiary might not be working. Future lump-sum expenses would include things like that new car down the line, university tuition fees for your children, money for vacations, and contingency funds."

"I have no idea how much a funeral costs," said Daniel, shaking his head.

"Let's estimate that it'll take between $10,000 and $15,000 to deal with all the costs associated with death and tying up your affairs," I suggested. "That should be more than enough."

Daniel wrote down $15,000 on his list.

"A new car, or a new used car, should cost another $15,000," suggested Lindsay. "But I don't know how to budget for university tuition."

"I'd add another $15,000," I said. "With an RESP — a registered education savings plan — the government will contribute money to your child's education as well. If you invest that $15,000 now, by the time your child is ready to go to university, the money will be there. We can talk about RESPs later, if you'd like. But remember, this is a hypothetical discussion — you've got to save for your child's education *outside* your insurance planning, too! You're hoping to be there to see the little tyke go off to college."

Daniel added the amounts for the car and tuition.

"As for vacations and contingency funds, that's up to you," I said. "If you're used to having nice holidays and want to maintain them with your insurance benefits, go ahead. And if you want a cash cushion, add it on. But I'm going to suggest that at your ages, and with your employment and earnings potential, you might be just fine without these extras. Yes, it would be devastating if one of you lost the other. But you're young enough and employable enough that either of you could go on with your careers in education and do quite well — well enough to finance your holidays and savings without the need of death benefits to do it for you. Life goes on."

"That's comforting," said Daniel. "Okay, zero for vacation and contingency, Linds?"

"Sounds good to me."

"Finally," I said, "you have to plan for inflation. Fifty thousand dollars a year seems like enough to live on now. But fifty grand a year in ten or fifteen years may not be enough to get by. I'm going to suggest that you don't worry too much about inflation at your ages, however. Again, life goes on. You've got lots of years of earning potential ahead of you to account for inflation, provided you invest your money wisely. As you get older, though, or if one of you is no longer in the workforce, I would factor in an amount for inflation."

Daniel now had several numbers written on the paper in front of him.

"Okay," I said, "we've accounted for the major needs if either of you dies prematurely. Let's add up the numbers."

Daniel began to do the tally. "Okay, $165,000 for income, plus the mortgage at $135,000. Fifteen grand respectively for our child's education, a new car, and death costs. My student loan at $9,000; Lindsay's at $5,000. The grand total is . . . $354,000 for me and $350,000 for Lindsay."

"Wait a sec," I said. "You upped your annual shortfall to $12,000 from $10,000. You'll need another $33,000 of insurance to make that up."

Daniel shook his head as he recalculated the figures. "Okay. The *new* grand total is $387,000 for me and $383,000 for Lindsay."

"Wow," said my niece. "So seven times my salary wasn't enough."

"No," I replied. "That's closer to ten times your salary."

She nodded.

"You've just figured out that you'll each need about $385,000 in life insurance," I said. "That's an appropriate amount for now. But please remember that your insurance needs will change over time. Your student loans will be paid off. You might have more children who will need to be fed, clothed, and educated, which probably means you'll need more coverage. And eventually, we hope those children will grow up and become self-sufficient, thereby eliminating an insurance need. You might buy a home, pay off a mortgage, divorce, remarry, change careers, get a big promotion, or win the lottery — although it's probably not a good idea to bank on that last one. Or you might find that with a careful savings and investment program, you've become self-insured — that is, your estate is sufficient on its own to replace any income lost as a result of premature death. I would suggest that you sit down and review your insurance needs every few years, or every time you make a major life change. You don't want too little coverage, and you don't want to have too much."

"But will we be able to afford that much insurance now?" asked Lindsay doubtfully. "That seems like an awful lot."

"You've forgotten something," I replied. "You're not going to have to buy the entire $385,000 worth of life insurance. Remember when I said you've got two life insurance policies you hadn't considered? Well, the second one is your benefit package at work. That should provide you with a fair amount of coverage. Usually, companies and unions offer life insurance to their members at very good rates. Do you know what your employers offer?"

"Um, I think I remember reading somewhere that they would pay us double our salary in death benefits," said my niece. "Hey, that's $70,000 right there!"

"That brings your needs down considerably," I said. "Now you're looking at buying closer to $315,000. Check with your human-resources manager or go through the literature that came with your benefit package. I'm sure your union offers life insurance coverage. Generally, though, there are limits on the amount of insurance you can purchase through union plans. You might have to go elsewhere to buy the full amount you need."

"How much do you think this will cost, anyway?" asked Lindsay.

"Given that you're both young, healthy non-smokers — and insurance companies charge considerably higher rates for smokers, by the way — I don't think it should be that expensive. In fact, I'll bet you could each get the coverage you need for around twenty-five dollars a month — maybe even less through your union's plan."

The surprise and relief on their faces was palpable.

"Really?" said Daniel. "I would have thought it would be

double or triple that. That's like two people going to see a movie a couple times a month."

"Plus the babysitter," added Lindsay. "We can afford fifty dollars a month."

"Especially when you realize what's at stake if you *don't* have insurance," I reminded them, at the risk of sounding preachy.

"So I make Daniel the beneficiary of my life insurance policy, and he makes me the beneficiary of his, right?" asked Lindsay.

"Correct. If you want, you can designate each other as irrevocable beneficiaries, which means that neither of you can change the beneficiary without the written consent of the other. A revocable beneficiary is one you can change at any time."

"Why would you want to change the beneficiary?" asked Daniel.

"If you separate or divorce, it might become an issue. I certainly hope you don't, but if — like your sister, Lisa, Lindsay — you find yourself dealing with the breakup of a marriage, it might be important to you to know that you still have life insurance on Daniel for the sake of your child. And vice versa, Daniel. Part of a divorce or separation agreement might stipulate that your ex, or your child, is the irrevocable beneficiary of your life insurance policy."

"Uncle Charles," said Lindsay, "what would happen if you had a couple where one partner made all the money? Would only the one with the income need life insurance?"

"Every situation is slightly different," I said, "but I would suggest that both partners should at least be insured for all the debt. If, for example, you — or Daniel — decided to quit your job and stay at home with the kids for the rest of your life, you'd probably still want a life insurance policy for the amount outstanding on your mortgage and student loans.

And you'd want to ensure that you had enough coverage to pay for child care in the event that the primary caregiver died.

"There's an opposite situation as well, now that you bring it up," I continued, "and that would be for a couple with children where both partners are very well off and don't really 'need' life insurance. The only hitch would be if they *both* died — say, in a car crash. Then their dependants would be in trouble if they didn't have any coverage. So they'd buy a policy that would pay out if they both died — usually that's called a joint last-to-die policy."

"Charles," said Daniel, "what happens if the insurance company where you have your policy goes bankrupt? Didn't that happen a few years back? If you'd had a policy with that company, what would have happened?"

"Ah, yes, Confederation Life. That surprised a lot of people. And Confederation wasn't a fly-by-night insurance company either. So, yes, it could happen that your insurance company goes out of business, although the chances of it happening are small. With Confederation Life and a couple of smaller insurance companies that also went out of business, other companies bought them and kept their clients' policies active. But even if that hadn't happened, insurance companies have their own form of insurance, if you will. There's an organization called COMPCORP — which stands for the Canadian Life and Health Insurance Compensation Corporation — that protects Canadian consumers of life and health insurance. If you have an insurance policy and the company you bought it from is a COMPCORP member, then your policy is automatically insured by COMPCORP. You don't have to buy extra insurance to cover your insurance!

"COMPCORP's coverage does have limits, though. It will cover up to $200,000 of life insurance and $60,000 of savings in various categories. So if you have an RRSP with a

COMPCORP member company, that would be covered for up to sixty grand. A non-registered savings account would also be covered up to the same limit, as would health insurance. COMPCORP also covers up to $2,000 a month for annuities, which we can talk about later, or disability income policies. So I wouldn't be too worried about your policy right now, as long as it's with a COMPCORP member company."

"Good," said Daniel.

"Another thing," I said. "You can help to protect your own investment by making sure that if you buy insurance through an agent, as opposed to your union, the agent you deal with is qualified and reputable. Get recommendations and references from your friends and colleagues. You could also call CAIFA — that's the Canadian Association of Insurance and Financial Advisors — and ask them to recommend a few agents in your area. Inquire about the agent's qualifications and ask to see proof of them. Ask to see his or her licence, and confirm the information with his or her office and even an advisory agency like CLHIA — the Canadian Life and Health Insurance Association. If you buy a policy, make sure there's a record of it with the company you buy it from. I know this may sound paranoid, but it never hurts. I've seen only four cases of insurance fraud in my forty years in this business, but each was devastating to the individuals involved. And no insurance professional will mind if you do your homework."

"What are the qualifications we're looking for?" asked Daniel.

"Well, all agents in Canada need a licence to sell insurance. And all agents need to spend a certain amount of time each year upgrading their education. Then there are industry-specific courses. Your agent might have, or be working towards getting, his or her certification as a chartered life underwriter and a chartered financial consultant — or CLU and ChFC, respectively. He or she might also be a certified financial planner, or CFP. What all these letters mean is that you're dealing with someone who has studied the industry and has passed qualifying examinations, and who's committed to educating him- or herself. But the most important thing is that you work with someone with whom you feel comfortable, who's professional and you can trust; lots of excellent agents don't become CLUs, financial planners, or the like, so it's not mandatory."

We looked up to the sound of the door opening once more. Catherine emerged onto the deck, carrying a mug of coffee.

"I was watching you three from the kitchen window," she said, smiling. "You were having such an intense conversation. Dare I ask what it was about?"

"You'll never guess, Mom," said Lindsay. "We're getting life insurance lessons!"

"Oh, I'm not surprised," my sister-in-law said. "Your Uncle Charles is one of the best people to talk to about insurance planning — your father and I learned everything we know from him. But am I interrupting?"

"I think we're just about done for this lesson," I suggested. "You now know what life insurance is, why you need it, and how much you need. Not bad for a couple hours. Next session, we can talk about the different kinds of life insurance and what the best type is for you."

"Not bad at all," said Lindsay. "Thank you so much, Uncle Charles!"

"Thanks, Charles," echoed Daniel. "This is really valuable information."

"My pleasure," I said. And it was.

"I think it's time for a second breakfast," said Lindsay. "After all this talk, I'm starving!"

RECIPES FOR SUCCESS

1   No amount of life insurance can ever
    replace the people you love — but it *can*
    help to ensure that your loved ones are
    protected financially, and can maintain
    their standard of living, in the event of your
    premature death.

2   How much life insurance do you need? A good rule of
    thumb is to multiply your gross income by five to seven.
    That'll give you a ballpark figure. (And remember that
    you might already have life insurance through
    government benefits and your employee plan.)

3   To get a more accurate assessment of your life
    insurance needs, you should complete a detailed
    needs assessment. See Appendix A for a sample.

4   Life goes on! Remember to review your life insurance
    needs every few years and with every major life change
    (like a marriage, divorce, new job, or new child).

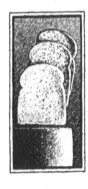

4

THE POLICY PARADIGM:

TERM, TERM-TO-100, AND PERMANENT INSURANCE

AH, cottage life! The morning unfolded into a glorious day. After breakfast, Lindsay and Daniel took off for a while in the powerboat while I decided to test out my canoeing skills, which I had sorely neglected. I managed to stern the craft a couple of times around the small lake before my arms started to complain.

I pulled the canoe onto the dock, where Catherine lay on a deck chair, reading. I could just catch her smile from underneath the wide brim of her sunhat.

"Having fun?" she asked.

"Lots," I replied. "It's great to be up here. What a wonderful way to start out retirement life."

"We're happy to have you here, too," she said. "And I have to say, I love what you're doing for Lindsay and Daniel. I was feeling a bit anxious about the two of them and their finances, especially with the baby on the way, but you're relieving my anxieties. I thought they didn't have enough insurance, but I don't like to interfere. You're a born teacher, though, Charles. They listen to you."

"I'm flattered," I said. "I have to admit, it's kind of nice to know I'm still useful."

"Useful?" She laughed. "Charles, your insurance advice alone is useful. But now that I know you can make cinnamon buns, you're *indispensable*."

"Wait till you try my focaccia," I told her.

◆ ◆ ◆

The following morning was beautiful, but by lunchtime, the sky had turned grey. As the first drops of rain began to fall, Lindsay and Daniel retreated inside to the kitchen, where I had just put the ingredients for focaccia into the breadmaker. Catherine followed them.

"I'm sorry it has to pour on your second day here," she said, "but I have to admit I love a good thunderstorm in the summer. It's so dramatic."

"It's okay," said Lindsay. "We've got work to do anyway. Uncle Charles, do you feel like continuing with the life insurance lesson?"

"I suppose *War and Peace* can wait," I said. "Great idea." I pressed the Start button. The machine clanked to life.

"I think I'll leave the three of you alone then," said Catherine. "Maybe I can convince your father to leave his computer and come watch the rain with me," she told Lindsay with a wink as she left the kitchen.

Lindsay, Daniel, and I sat down at the kitchen table.

"Where did we leave off last time?" I asked.

"We figured out how much insurance we need," said Daniel.

"Right! So now you need to know what kind to get," I mused.

"I didn't know there were different kinds *to* get," remarked Lindsay.

"Oh, yes," I told her. "There's a mind-numbing array of insurance products out there, and more come onto the market all the time. But when it comes right down to it, there are really only two types of insurance: term and permanent. Everything else, in my opinion, is a variation on those two types, or a combination of them."

"What's the difference?" asked Daniel.

"Let me give you an analogy that I've used for my clients in the past. You guys have been living in rented apartments for most of your adult lives, right?"

"Right," said Lindsay. "But we'd really like to buy something soon."

"Well, if you'd like to buy something, what's preventing you?"

"Money," they answered simultaneously.

"Exactly," I said. "You'd like to buy a house, but the costs of buying, at least initially, tend to be much more expensive than those of renting. Not only are there mortgage payments to be made each month, but you have to come up with a hefty down payment. You have to pay property taxes and land-transfer taxes, as well as legal fees. And when the furnace breaks down or the roof caves in, you can't call your landlord at two in the morning to get it fixed. It's your responsibility."

"It makes me wonder why we're so gung-ho about buying," mused Daniel.

"There are a lot of good reasons to buy, too," I said. "Things like building up equity, security, pride in ownership. But let's take a look at your apartment. What are your costs there?"

"We pay rent and utilities," said Lindsay, "but that's it."

"And do those costs go up or are they fixed?"

"Well, they're fixed according to the terms of the lease, but the landlord can raise the rent by a certain percentage every year."

"So over time, your costs go up for the same product."

"Right," said Daniel.

"Well, the difference between term insurance and permanent insurance is a lot like the difference between renting and owning your home. When you rent, your costs are lower than if you buy, especially at the outset. They'll go up over time, because of inflation or because you decide to rent a bigger apartment or move to a more expensive area of town. Eventually, your rental costs might get to be expensive enough that you wonder if it's smarter to buy. In Toronto, for example, the cost of renting is so high right now that many young people who can scrape together the down payment feel they're better off buying.

"But the thing about renting," I continued, "is that once you leave an apartment, you leave with nothing. You've paid your rent, and you've had shelter while you've paid it, but that's where it ends. Your rent hasn't given you any ownership in the place."

"I *hate* that," said Lindsay. "Sometimes I think about the fact that I could be paying all this money into a house that I actually own."

"On the other hand," I said, "you couldn't really have afforded to buy a home all those years you were renting, so renting was a good alternative — maybe even the only alternative, aside from living with your parents or on the street. It allowed you to free up that down payment for other things: like tuition, your wedding, travel, a car."

"That's true," said Daniel.

"Term insurance is similar to renting an apartment," I said. "It's a comparatively inexpensive way of protecting your dependants in case of your premature death, just as renting can be a relatively inexpensive way of providing shelter in comparison with owning a home, at least in the early years of home ownership. When you rent, you sign a lease for a specific amount of time, and you pay rent every month to keep that lease in force. When you buy term insurance, you buy a policy for a specified amount of time — usually one, five, ten, or twenty years — and you pay the premiums, or the cost of keeping the policy in force, for that term."

"Which is where the name comes from," said Lindsay.

"Exactly. And at the end of that term, the policy ends. You haven't built up any equity in that policy, just as you don't own the apartment at the end of your lease. It's the bare-bones version of insurance.

"And," I continued, "in the same way that your rental costs go up over time, so does the cost of term insurance. Care to take a guess as to why?"

"Isn't it that we're getting older?" asked Lindsay after a pause. "Life insurance is supposed to protect your dependants in the case of premature death, right? So the younger you are, the less likely it is that you'll die prematurely. You're not as great a risk to the insurance company, so it can charge you less. But as you get older, your chance of dying prematurely increases, so the company charges you more to cover its butt."

"I wouldn't have put it exactly that way," I said, smiling, "but you've hit the nail on the head. There's also a form of term insurance often called term-to-100, which is essentially a permanent form of term insurance. Some folks refer to it as perma-term for that very reason. Term-to-100 would be like signing a lifetime lease on an apartment at a set rent. As long as you paid the rent, you'd have shelter. And with perma-term, as long as you paid the premiums, you'd have life insurance coverage. But with most term-to-100 policies, you wouldn't build up any savings, or equity, in the policy, just as at the end of your lease, the apartment wouldn't belong to you. And of course, your rent, or your premiums, would be higher than they would be if you signed a lease for a shorter period, because the landlord would have to factor in inflation and the rising value of the property over time.

"Now, there is a point at which you can no longer buy term insurance, usually at around age seventy-five or eighty, depending on the insurance company. You're just too much of a risk to make it worthwhile for insurance companies to sell you a term policy at rates you could afford. What are the odds of a seventy-five-year-old man dying within ten or fifteen years?"

"So," asked Daniel, "am I correct in assuming that if term insurance is like renting an apartment, and term-to-100 is like a lifetime rental, then permanent insurance is the equivalent of buying a house?"

"You are — to a certain extent," I answered. "But here's where you need to be careful with the analogy."

"Why?" asked Lindsay.

"Because buying a house and buying an insurance policy aren't the same, even if they do make for a nice analogy. Just because one day you'd like to own your own home doesn't mean that it's necessarily the wisest financial decision, even if it's the right one emotionally. There's a lot of emotion tied up in both purchases, and you need to make sure that you're buying each one for the reasons that best suit your financial *and* emotional needs.

"And," I continued, "just because you like the idea of owning your home better than renting it, that doesn't mean that you should assume that permanent insurance is a better option than term insurance. But some people make the mistake I warned you about — thinking of permanent insurance in *exactly* the same way they would a house. They feel like they're somehow 'throwing away' those premium payments when they buy term insurance because they don't get anything at the end of the policy."

"That's the way I feel about paying rent," said Lindsay, sighing.

"There are a couple of problems with that line of reasoning, however," I countered. "One is that they're forgetting that those premiums they paid actually did get them something they needed: coverage at a low cost. In the same way, I would argue you're not 'throwing away' money every time you write a rent cheque. You get shelter at a reasonable cost

— at least in most Canadian cities — by paying rent, and that's one of life's basic necessities."

I was getting warmed up now.

"You have to keep in mind your reasons for buying life insurance — in your case, it's primarily about ensuring your family's financial security. So it's important not to get caught in the trap of thinking that your insurance coverage is worthless if it's not also an investment vehicle. But I'm getting ahead of myself here. Let's go over how permanent — or, as it's sometimes called, 'whole life' — insurance works. Can either one of you take a stab at it?"

"Okay," said Daniel. "You've just explained that term insurance is similar to renting an apartment. When you rent, you're paying for shelter only, and so it's cheaper than owning a house. And it's only temporary. So my guess is that permanent insurance policies cover you for life, that they're more expensive than term, and that you must get more for your premiums than just coverage — that investment component you've been talking about."

"That's it in a nutshell," I replied. "When you buy a permanent, or 'whole life,' policy —"

"— which covers you for your whole life," Lindsay interjected.

"Correct. Again, hence the name. When you buy that policy, the insurance company charges you a higher premium than it does for term. And that premium is usually level — that is, unlike term insurance, it'll cost you the same amount when you're twenty years old as it will when you're sixty. Essentially, what the insurance company does is spread the cost of insuring you over the course of your life and divide that amount into equal premium payments. It then takes part of that premium and puts it in what's known as a reserve, where it grows over the years. This is what's known as the cash value of the policy. The growing reserve account is one reason the premiums remain level, as opposed to increasing in the policy's later years, when they would otherwise increase to reflect your greater likehood of dying. If you cancel your policy, you get the built-up cash value. If you die, your beneficiaries get the death benefits, but in many policies, they won't necessarily receive the cash value. That belongs to the insurance company."

"So it's one or the other, but not both," clarified Daniel.

"Usually," I said. "Policies will vary, though. You can also take out what's known as a policy loan against the cash value if you need the money. In the past, some permanent policies came with a guaranteed policy loan. That meant that you could borrow money from your policy at a guaranteed low rate of interest, like 6 percent. In the 1980s, however, interest rates for even safe investments were much higher than that, around 20 percent. So people took advantage of the low rates; they borrowed money from their policies at the low rates and invested it for a much higher rate of return. I used to help clients use their guaranteed policy loans all the time. Unfortunately, those kinds of loan provisions ended a good thirty years ago."

"No fair," muttered Lindsay.

"Life ain't fair, my darling niece," I told her.

"Whole life doesn't seem so bad," said Lindsay. "You get the death benefit if you die, and you get the cash value if you live and cancel the policy — the best of both worlds. And you still have a loan available."

"It's not so bad," I said, "unless you can invest your money on your own and get a better return on it. There's a saying in the finance industry: 'buy term and invest the difference' — the difference being the difference in cost for the two policies. It's not bad advice. If you did that and invested your money wisely, you might come out ahead. The problem is that most people *don't* invest the difference. They lack the discipline. So whole life becomes a forced savings plan for them that ensures they sock away some cash every month or year. I've had clients in the past who told me, in no uncertain terms, that they wanted to buy permanent rather than term because they wouldn't save any money otherwise, and that they wanted 'something to show' for the premiums they paid if they cancelled the policy down the road, or if they needed a loan. As for the cash value, while it's nice to have a loan available, remember that, depending on the policy, your beneficiaries may receive *only* the death benefits, not the cash value. In fact, that cash reserve isn't yours — it belongs to the insurance company."

"That makes it exactly like term insurance, doesn't it?" asked Daniel.

"You're catching on," I said. "Both policies, in general, will pay out only a death benefit if you die. Term is the simpler bet with your insurance company: if you die before the term is up, they'll pay the death benefit. If you don't, you get nothing. With permanent insurance, if you die, you get the death benefit. But if you live, the extra costs have given you the flexibility of borrowing on the policy by way of a policy loan, as well as the option of cancelling the policy outright and getting the money in your reserve account. Those are selling points for some people. But there's nothing to prevent you from investing the difference on your own outside the policy. That way, you'd have both insurance coverage *and* cash savings.

"As well," I continued, "it generally takes quite a while, say a good ten years, for the cash value inside the policy to build up to any significant amount. The insurance company needs to cover its issue costs in the first few years of your policy, and those costs — like taxes and acquisition expenses — come out of the first premiums you pay. Those costs, by the way, are there for term insurance as well. But in that case, they're lower, in part because the insurance company's costs, and its risk, are lower with term insurance: they're counting on the fact that most people won't die before the term ends.

"As for being able to get a loan from your policy," I went on, "that could come in handy if you need some money quickly. You might even be able to get a lower interest rate than you would at a bank, or you could receive a loan with less hassle and paperwork. If you die while the loan is out-standing, however, the company might have the right to deduct the amount payable from your death benefit.

"Now, some permanent policies are called participating policies, because, as the name suggests, the insurance com-pany feels that you're participating in its financial life. With this type of policy, the company will pay you a dividend — that is, money — which you can leave in your policy to build up in that reserve account, take as cash, use to reduce your premiums, or even use to buy more insurance. Usually, the company pays dividends according to a scale that's predeter-mined when the policy is issued. But you have to be careful: these kinds of policies are generally more expensive than non-participating policies, which don't pay dividends, because the company has to charge more to provide for the dividend. Also, the dividend amount isn't guaranteed. It can be higher or lower, depending on the company's financial year."

"So why do people buy permanent policies instead of term?" asked Lindsay.

"Well, for a number of reasons. First of all, there may be a point at which the premiums for term insurance become too expensive, or you're too old to qualify for it. Generally, the maximum age is eighty. Another reason is that some people like to know what they'll be paying for insurance for the rest of their lives. They know they'll pay, say, forty-five dollars a month, every month, for as long as they keep the policy in force. It's a done deal for them. And when you think about it, the cost for the premium actually decreases over time because of inflation. The forty-five dollars you pay now will be worth a lot less than the forty-five dollars you pay in twenty years."

"But, Charles," said Daniel, "if you want to know what you'll be paying for the rest of your life, couldn't you just buy a term-to-100 policy? The same holds true for those premiums decreasing, doesn't it?"

"It does," I answered. "That's one strategy that would work quite nicely if you wanted to know your future costs but didn't want to buy permanent insurance. But another reason that people like permanent insurance, one that won't hold with perma-term, is that eventually some whole-life policies can be paid off in full. Then, even when you're not paying the premiums, you're still insured for life. There's something attractive in that to people; they like knowing that they 'own' the policy, and that they're insured for life no matter what. If I can go back to the 'apartment versus house' analogy, it's similar to paying off your mortgage: at some point the house is yours, free and clear.

"Similarly, if you've already had a permanent policy for fifteen or twenty years, it might just make sense to keep it. Over time, your dividends, or the cash value in the policy, might eventually grow to the point where they generate enough interest to cover your premiums. This is the famous 'vanishing premium' trick, and it's a nice bonus for policyholders, who no longer have to pay out-of-pocket costs for their policies. But there's no guarantee that this will happen. For a while, for example, insurance companies were selling so-called premium-offset policies, which promised, in exchange for a larger premium at the beginning, to eventually pay for themselves. But when interest rates went down, some buyers were pretty shocked to find that their policies would take more than forty-five years to become self-funding!"

"That's a pretty slow vanishing act," said Daniel.

"Yup," I said. "The rules around those kinds of guarantees are much tighter now. But to continue answering your question, Lindsay, some people — and insurance professionals — believe that you should use term insurance to cover temporary needs and permanent insurance to cover permanent needs. According to that theory, you'd use term insurance to cover your mortgage or your children's education, or your need for lots of coverage when you've got young, dependent children. And you'd use permanent insurance to cover expenses that won't go away over time, like your funeral expenses, income taxes after death, or the needs of a disabled child who might be dependent on you for his or her lifetime."

"That seems to make sense," nodded Daniel.

"It has pros and cons as a philosophy," I said. "On the one hand, it's clear that some financial needs are temporary and others are permanent, and there is some logic in the idea that you should have permanent coverage for the permanent needs. Some people enjoy the peace of mind of knowing that their permanent needs will always be covered, as long as they pay their premiums. It's an individual choice, I suppose. There's nothing to say, however, that you can't just renew your term policy to cover the permanent needs, but your term costs might become very high as you get older."

"Once again, couldn't you just buy perma-term?" asked Lindsay.

"You could," I said, nodding. "Another way to think about it is that your goal might eventually be to become self-insured. If you're disciplined about saving and investing, you might eventually reach the point where your savings — what's known as your estate — are sufficient to cover your permanent needs. When you become self-insured, you don't really need insurance, permanent or temporary, although you may buy it for estate planning and the like. But we can talk about those later. Take me, for example. There will be funeral costs and income tax to pay upon my death, but my estate — that is, my savings and investments — is large enough to easily cover those expenses. Why would I buy any kind of life insurance for the purpose of covering expenses I can already afford?"

"Hey!" said Daniel. "You know what I just realized? I think I *have* a whole-life policy. I'm pretty sure that my parents took out insurance policies on me and my brother when we were kids. It's for around $10,000."

"You've probably got a few thousand dollars' worth of cash value in that policy by now," I pointed out.

"You know, I never realized there *was* cash value in that policy," mused Daniel. "I wonder if it's worth cashing in."

"It might just be," I said. "You need much more insurance than $10,000 now anyway. If you've got a few thousand dollars in the policy, you could cash it in and even use the money to help pay for the term insurance that you and Lindsay need. You could even put the balance into an RRSP. You should do some research on it and see exactly what the policy comprises."

"That's a great idea!" said Daniel. "Thanks, Charles!"

"One thing to remember, though," I cautioned. "Don't cancel or cash in that permanent policy — *any* policy, for that matter — until you've got the new one in hand."

"Why not?" asked Lindsay.

"Think about it," I replied. "You cancel the old policy for $10,000 and apply for your $270,000 of life insurance. And as you're applying, Daniel gets hit by a bus. Or you go for the medical exam and find out that —"

"He has terminal cancer and only a few months to live," Lindsay cheerfully finished my sentence.

"Great," said Daniel morosely.

"Exactly. Sad and unlikely, but possible. The death benefit of the old policy may not seem like much in comparison with the life insurance you've figured out you need, but it's certainly better than the few thousand dollars you'd get by cashing it in. And remember, the death benefit is tax-free, but you may have to pay taxes on the cash value. So do yourselves a favour and always wait until the new policy's in place before getting rid of the old one."

"Maybe I'll phone my parents and see what they think," said Daniel. "I bet they'll be surprised."

"They probably will," I replied.

"Well, we won't be buying any life insurance on this baby!" said Lindsay, patting her belly.

"I think that's a fine decision," I said. "Children *are* dependants; they don't *have* dependants. So, generally, they don't need life insurance. But I should point out that you do have a couple of options when it comes to life insurance for your kids."

"Like what?" asked Daniel.

"Well, you can get a rider on your policy that covers your child for anywhere between $2,000 and $20,000. A rider is just optional term protection for a specific situation, like insuring your child. The kind of rider I'm talking about covers all your children, even those who haven't yet been born, from age zero to twenty years. Coverage takes effect on the fifteenth day of life, and generally pays out only 50 percent of the death benefit until the child is six months old."

"Why?" asked Daniel.

"Mostly because of the risk of sudden infant death syndrome — SIDS," I said.

"But if kids don't have dependants, why would they need the life insurance, even as a rider?" asked Lindsay. "Aren't you contradicting yourself here?"

"Not really," I said. "This insurance is less about protecting dependants than it is about guaranteeing the future insurability of your child. You see, these riders are very inexpensive. You could probably get one for a few dollars a month, so it's really a very small investment for you. But until they reach twenty-five, the insured children can convert their riders into permanent insurance policies for up to five times the amount you've covered them for — with no medical exam. So a $20,000 rider can turn into a $100,000 policy. This would come in handy if there were future health issues. Say your child developed a serious medical condition that would make buying life insurance more difficult later on in life. He or she would have the option of converting the rider and guaranteeing some insurability."

"Oh," said Daniel, "so it's just a way of making sure that your kid will be able to get at least some life insurance coverage down the line."

"Exactly," I said. "And it does provide some insurance coverage in the meantime. It's just one more option for you to consider."

"So it looks as though we're investigating buying term insurance," said Daniel.

"I think that's probably the best choice for you at this stage in your lives," I replied. "You're young, soon-to-be parents with high life insurance needs and not much disposable income. But when you buy your term policies, it's very important that you make sure you can eventually convert those policies into permanent policies, if necessary. Actually, when you buy term, make sure that it's both *convertible* and *renewable*."

"What's the difference?" asked Lindsay.

"'Renewable' means that you can renew the policy when the term is up, without a medical examination. That's important. At the end of your twenty-year term, you'll both be in your fifties. A medical exam then could turn up health problems you might have developed between now and then, and those problems could make you a bad risk for insurance, or even ineligible for coverage. So buying a renewable policy, even if it is a bit more expensive than a non-renewable one, is always a good idea. It means that you can renew at the rates charged to an average customer your age — not someone with, say, a life-threatening medical condition. Of course, you two take great care of yourselves, so let's hope the odds of you developing those conditions are low. Still, it's better to be safe than sorry.

"Now, even if your policy is guaranteed renewable," I continued, "it might not guarantee that the premiums you'll pay in the future won't be exorbitant. If you want to play it really safe, you can buy a policy that gives you a guaranteed premium rate upon renewal. Again, this type of policy might be slightly more expensive, but if you'll sleep better at night knowing what you'll be paying in twenty years, it's something to consider."

"Okay, renewable it is," said Lindsay. "I guess we'd have to see what the rates are for a guaranteed premium. And you also said something about convertible insurance."

"Yes, I did. Convertible term insurance is exactly what it sounds like: when you buy your term policy, you want to make sure that when it ends, you can convert it to a permanent policy — either whole life or something called universal life, which we'll talk about later — again without a medical exam. For this reason, you might want to make sure that the company you buy from actually offers various kinds of permanent policies. There's no point in having convertible insurance if there's nothing to convert it into. Also, many insurance companies have a maximum age at which you can convert a term policy — usually around fifty-five or sixty. So check out the age limit for conversion when you buy your term policy."

"Why would we want to convert to permanent insurance?" asked Lindsay.

"Well, for a few reasons," I replied. "First, you may as well have all the flexibility you can. Most term policies *are* guaranteed convertible, so it won't cost you much, if anything, in terms of increased premiums. And some of the reasons for buying permanent insurance that we've already discussed might just appeal to you in ten or twenty years.

But I think the most important reason for making sure you have convertible insurance is that some newer permanent policies — those universal life policies — are a potentially excellent investment. They're a relatively new breed of permanent life insurance that combines the benefits of term with more competitive rates of return, plus tax advantages. When you've paid off your debts, have a little more disposable income, and have managed to put more money into your RRSPs, come back to me and we'll talk about universal life insurance."

I paused. "You do know what an RRSP — a registered retirement savings plan — is, don't you?"

"It's okay, Charles," said Daniel. "We're not completely lost causes. We know about RRSPs, although we haven't been very good about putting money into them."

"I suppose a refresher course in RRSPs wouldn't be a bad thing either," mused Lindsay.

"That's a whole other lesson," I replied. "I'm a firm believer that RRSPs and related investments like those RESPs we've been talking about are just as much a part of life insurance as a term policy is. But we can discuss those later — no need to make this conversation more complicated."

"Okay," said Daniel. "So we need to get two term policies for about $270,000 each, depending on how much coverage we have through our union."

"Two hundred and seventy thousand dollars," mused Lindsay, getting that devilish look I recognized from her youth, "plus whatever we get from work. Hey, Daniel, what if I hired a hit man and —"

"Not so fast, young lady," I admonished her. "If you have him killed and you get caught, you won't get a penny of the insurance proceeds."

"Guess I'd better let you live then," said Lindsay, poking her incredibly good-natured husband.

"While we're on the subject, did you know that if you commit suicide and your policy has been in force for less than two years, it's automatically nullified?"

"Really?" asked Lindsay, all traces of devilishness now gone.

"Really. In fact, if you die within two years of taking out a policy, the insurance company will check to make sure that the death was not a suicide. It's a way, I suppose, of preventing someone who is desperate or very depressed from buying a policy and then killing him- or herself the next day. It protects both the consumer and the insurance company, although it's certainly one of the more macabre aspects of life insurance."

"Are there more macabre details?" asked Lindsay, still intrigued.

"Well, there are a few more interesting bits. For instance, you have to have an 'insurable interest' in taking out a policy on someone's life. Now, you and Daniel, as a married couple, obviously have important reasons for having insurance policies on each other. As spouses, you're what's known as preferred beneficiaries to each other. Your child will also be a preferred beneficiary. But you would have no insurable interest in a stranger off the street, and you couldn't buy a policy on that stranger. In the same way, any reputable insurance company would be very, very wary of, say, average-income parents buying a million-dollar policy on their young child. Or of a low-income man buying a few million dollars' worth of life insurance on his estranged wife. Lindsay, I know — at least I hope! — you were joking about offing Daniel for the insurance money, but sad to say, some people do see a big insurance payout as a reason for murder. You hear about it a lot more in movies and detective novels than you do in real life, but it has been known to happen. People who sell life insurance have to make sure that their customers have what's known as a proper financial and/or moral understanding in the policies they buy."

"You were talking about a rider for insuring your kids, Uncle Charles," said Lindsay. "What other kinds of riders are there?"

"Oh, lots," I said. "For example, there's something called double indemnity, which will pay double if you get killed in an accident instead of dying of natural causes. It's usually known today as an accidental-death benefit."

"What's the point of that?" asked Daniel. "I mean, once you're dead, you're dead, right? Why would it make a difference if you died in an accident or by natural causes?"

"I agree," I said. "In any case, fewer than 10 percent of all deaths of adults aged twenty-five to sixty-five are the result of accidents. One rider I think *is* potentially interesting is called a waiver of premium. It means that if you're disabled, your insurance premiums are automatically waived for the duration of the disability. That could be useful if your income is reduced because of your disability. On the other hand, you have to look at what the insurance company considers a disability. You may want to look into a disability policy instead, but we can discuss that a different day as well."

"Okay," said Daniel. "Any thoughts on how long a term we should sign up for?"

"That's up to you," I said. "With a child, or children, to raise, you're going to need coverage for quite some time. I would say that the least amount of time you probably want is ten years, and then you can renew for another ten, if that's what you want. Or you could buy a twenty-year term policy and be done with it. By that time, your insurance needs, and your overall financial picture, will probably have changed considerably. If I were you, I'd probably go with the renewable, convertible ten-year term. There are so many good products out there that you might want to switch over earlier than you imagine. But research the different policies and decide for yourself."

"How do we find a policy?" asked Lindsay. "Hey, Uncle Charles, can we do it through you?"

"Nope," I said. "Even if I wasn't retired — which I am, I have to keep reminding myself — I'd probably send you to someone else if you came to me to buy life insurance. Actually, I know a very good broker in Ottawa. I'll give you her name."

"Why shouldn't we use you?" asked Lindsay.

"For a couple reasons. First, you have to disclose a lot of personal, medical, and financial information to your insurance agent or broker, and that's not necessarily the kind of information you want to tell me. Second, what if you weren't happy with the service I provided? You'd have a hard time firing me and then showing up at Thanksgiving dinner with me the next month."

Lindsay laughed.

"Most important, although I hate to admit it, I'm too old for you. Think about it: this is a purchase that's going to last you for a very long time. You want your agent or broker to be of your generation — in the same way that you want your family doctor to age with you. Someone your age will most likely have a better grasp of your needs and lifestyle, and he or she will hopefully be around as you age to advise you on future decisions."

"So where should we find that broker?" asked Daniel.

"The same way you'd find any other professional — ask friends and colleagues who have bought insurance, check references, and interview a few people until you find someone you feel comfortable with and can trust."

"Is that how it works — you find this agent or broker, and he or she sells you insurance?" asked Lindsay.

"Pretty much. Today, you can buy life insurance from banks and credit card companies, as well as the more traditional insurance companies. But in general, there are three ways to buy: from an agent or broker who works for one company and sells that company's product; from a broker who deals with a range of companies; or through a call centre or the Internet, where you phone in or fill in an application on-line, and somebody representing the company calls you back and completes the deal from there. Actually, make that three and a half ways. You can often buy it through alumni and professional associations; just call them up, and they'll send you an application form."

"Where do we begin?" My niece looked a bit put off.

"Well, I'd suggest you do your homework. Find out how much life insurance your union offers, and get their rates for more life insurance. But I would suggest that you don't rely only on your union's plan — there are usually caps on how much you can buy, and your benefits could change the next time you negotiate a collective agreement."

"I hadn't thought of that," remarked Daniel.

"You can also check out the rates from group plans from alumni or professional associations. You might see if your university has an alumni life insurance plan, with lower rates. Some of these plans, however, offer only non-convertible term insurance, so keep that in mind if you're looking for a convertible policy.

"Also, get on-line to one of those new web sites that can give you a comparison of different life insurance rates — in fact, we can go bother your father right now and have a look."

We all trooped into Peter's little den. To our surprise, he wasn't parked in front of his computer.

"That's right!" said Lindsay. "Mom must have got him to take a walk in the rain with her."

"Your father's really a romantic at heart," I said, grinning. "Okay, let's have a look here."

I sat down in front of the computer, opened the Internet browser, and connected. As we waited for the connection, I continued to talk.

"What we're doing here is getting a sense of how much a ten-year term policy should cost for each of you. You don't necessarily want to go with the lowest rate or the companies that the search engine will generate, but you do want to get a sense of how much different companies charge for term insurance, and if it's renewable and convertible. If a rate is much higher or much lower than the others, I would want to know why."

I typed "term insurance quotes" and "+ Canada" into Peter's search engine, and the computer came up with a list of web sites. I clicked one at random for the purposes of demonstration.

"Okay, now we need to fill in the information. What are the first three letters of your postal code?"

"K2L," said Lindsay.

"Okay. Daniel, when's your birthday?"

"December 10, 1968," he answered.

"Ah, a Sagittarian." I typed that in, clicked "no" to the question that asked if Daniel used tobacco, and rated his health as "preferred."

"Let's choose a ten-year guaranteed term policy for $300,000," I said. I hit the "compare now" button on the screen. Up popped a list of annual rates for the policy. They ranged between $225 and $350.

"That's not bad," said Daniel.

"Let's do me now," said Lindsay.

"Won't her costs be the same?" asked Daniel. "I mean, we're the same age."

"Watch," I said. I typed in Lindsay's birthday — April 18, 1968 — and clicked on "female." The table popped up again. This time the premiums ranged from $200 to $325.

"Why does she cost less to insure than me?" asked Daniel.

Lindsay just grinned.

"It's all actuarial tables," I said. "Women are less likely to die prematurely than men. They have a longer lifespan, so they cost less per year to insure. It all tends to even out in the end, though: because women tend to live longer, they'll pay premiums for a longer time before a death benefit is paid."

Now Daniel grinned.

"Anyway, now you have an idea of how much you'll probably spend. You can even click here for names of agents. But as I said, the best way to find a good broker is through word of mouth. When you meet with a potential broker or agent, make sure you feel comfortable before you proceed any further. Ask lots of questions, and make sure that the person you eventually hire is qualified and educated."

"Right," said Daniel.

"Also remember that once you have the policy in hand, you have ten days to change your mind and nullify the deal. That's standard across the industry."

"Do you have to have a medical exam to buy insurance?" asked Lindsay.

"It depends on the company and the policy, and how much insurance you're buying," I replied, "but for insurance coverage of more than $100,000, you can generally expect some kind of medical exam. When you apply for insurance, you'll have to fill out a bunch of detailed questionnaires that ask about your health — physical and mental — as well as family histories. They're also going to want to know about your personal life. Do you have a criminal record? Have you ever used recreational drugs? Do you have any dangerous hobbies, like scuba diving or bungee jumping?"

"What if" — Daniel looked a bit uncomfortable — "you've, uh . . ."

"Smoked a joint or two in college?" I asked.

"Yeah," he said, reddening.

"Tell the truth on the application. They're not asking so that they can penalize you for what you did ten years ago. They just want to get a sense of the kinds of risks you might have taken in the past or are still taking. There's a big difference, at least in terms of buying life insurance, between taking a couple of tokes in a frat house and a thousand-dollar-a-day cocaine habit. You don't want to lie on the application form. If they find out that you lied, it could nullify the policy. Don't worry."

"Okay," he said. "Thanks, Charles."

"Because you guys are young and healthy, and aren't getting a million-dollar policy, the insurance company may just require a statement from you and your doctor saying that you're in good health, plus a visit from a paramedic or a nurse to check your height and weight and your blood pressure. If you're buying a lot of coverage, or you're not in good health, you may need a full physical, even EKGs and CAT scans, if the company deems it necessary. Every policy is different, and it's up to the company or broker to decide what health criteria they need to sell you a policy."

"What if you get turned down after a medical examination?"

"It's not likely that you would be. For the two of you, qualifying for life insurance shouldn't be a problem. You're young, healthy, active, and you don't smoke. Your premiums will be lower than those of a smoker who isn't active — that's called preferred underwriting, and you should ask whomever you buy insurance from if he or she will give you a break on your premiums because you have a healthy lifestyle. In any case, only about 4 percent of people are refused outright when they try to buy life insurance policies, usually because they have pre-existing health problems. Nobody's going to sell life insurance to somebody with terminal cancer or someone who's had a couple of heart bypasses, for example."

"What if you've got a family history of disease?" asked Daniel. "I know that a lot of the women on my father's side of the family have had breast cancer. Can they refuse to cover you if they think you might be at higher risk?"

"They can," I said, "but generally they won't. If they excluded everyone who had a family history of *something*, there wouldn't be very many people left to insure. What insurance companies do is share the risk; they assume that some of their clients will inherit terminal diseases, and they price their policies to account for that risk. That's all insurance — of any kind — really is: pooling risk. If you disclosed to an insurance company that there's a high rate of breast cancer in your family, the company might want to give you a 'rated' or 'extra-risk' policy, at a slightly higher rate per thousand dollars of coverage.

"What's interesting, though, is the idea of genetic testing. That's something my generation never thought of, but yours will have to deal with. When Anne was undergoing treatment for cancer, the clinic and the hospital had genetic research programs that tested for the gene mutations for breast and ovarian cancer. If a woman has those mutations, she will in some cases have up to a 95 percent chance of developing cancer. Now, if a woman was tested for those mutations and found that she had them, she might have a very difficult time getting life insurance."

"That's scary," said Lindsay.

"It's not the most comforting thought," I agreed. "If I was deciding whether to undergo genetic testing for a disease, I'd want to make sure I had a solid, renewable policy at a guaranteed rate *before* I got the test. For that matter, I'd also want to make sure I had damn good disability insurance, too, if I needed it. If you find out bad news, then at least you know you'll be covered in the event of premature death or disability."

The bread-maker began its now-familiar pinging sound. I stood up from the computer and stretched.

"That, my pupils, is the bell. Class dismissed. I have to make focaccia now."

RECIPES FOR SUCCESS

1 When it comes right down to it, there are just two types of life insurance: term and permanent. Everything else is just a variation, or combination, of these two.

2 The difference between term and permanent insurance is a lot like the difference between renting and owning your home. With term, you sign a contract for a specific amount of time and pay premiums for the length of the contract. As you get older, your premium costs will go up. When the contract ends, so does your insurance coverage. With permanent insurance, your coverage lasts your entire life and your premiums are usually level. Permanent policies also have a cash value. If you cancel the policy, you get the cash value.

3 "Buy term and invest the difference." To follow that advice, buy (usually) less expensive term coverage and invest the amount you've saved in premium costs. This way, you've taken advantage of both lower insurance costs and the benefits of investing.

4 Play it safe: don't cancel or cash in an old life insurance policy until you've got the new one in hand.

5 When you buy term insurance, it's a good idea to make sure your coverage is both *renewable* and *convertible*.

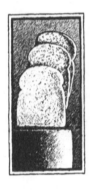

5

It's Universal:

Life Insurance for the Next Generation

"**G**RANDPA! Grandma! We're here!"

I had just taken a seven-grain honey loaf out of the bread-maker and placed it on the baker's rack to cool when I heard a car door slam, followed by the sound that brings joy to every grandparent's face: the voice of a grandchild.

Ah, I thought, Andrew and Rebecca and the kids must have arrived.

Andrew is my nephew, Peter and Catherine's second child and only son. Growing up as the only male child in a house full of daughters, however, didn't afford him any special treatment from his parents. He washed dishes and helped with the housework, just like his sisters. They, in turn, helped rake leaves, mow the lawn, and shovel snow. In the end, I think having three sisters has been a blessing for Andrew; it's given him a healthy respect for, and comfort around, women. As he once said to me, "All my sisters were good at stuff — sports, school, the arts. It would have been stupid to try to say that boys were better. Anyway, they would've beat me up if I'd tried."

Andrew's sound judgement is reflected in his choice of a

life partner: his wife, Rebecca. She's cut from the same cloth as my nieces — athletic, smart, and a go-getter. She's in sales, working for a pharmaceutical company. He works for Bell Canada as an account representative. Together, they're great parents to their two kids, Alexandra, who's eight, and four-year-old Jack. They live in a Montreal suburb and were taking a July long weekend to visit the family cottage.

I joined the rest of the extended Stonehouse clan on the front porch. Alex had been the first to emerge from the car, and she was chattering away excitedly to her grandparents, who, in turn, were thrilled to see her. Andrew unstrapped Jack from his car seat, and he too made a beeline for Grandma and Grandpa.

"There's my Jack-in-the-box!" crowed Peter, lifting Jack high into the air. The little boy shrieked with laughter.

"They've grown so much," I said to Andrew and Rebecca after we hugged hello. I hadn't seen them or the kids since New Year's, which I'd spent at Peter and Catherine's house in Ottawa. "Jack's at least a couple of inches taller. And Alex, where are your front teeth?"

My grandniece flashed a gape-toothed grin at me. "I got five dollars," she said, "from the tooth fairy."

Rebecca pointed at Andrew when Alex wasn't looking.

"Grandma, Grandpa, I want to go swimming in the lake," said Alexandra. "I can do the front crawl now, and diving!"

"I want to play in the sandbox!" said Jack, tugging on the hem of Rebecca's shorts.

"How about we all have some lunch first?" suggested Rebecca. "You guys must need to eat something, and then we can play."

"Yes, indeed," said Peter, scooping up his granddaughter and carrying her, giggling, into the kitchen. "We'll all have something to eat, and then Grandma and I can take you swimming, and Jack can play in the sandbox."

"And you and Rebecca can relax after your drive," added

Catherine. "There's beer in the fridge, and Charles has just made more wonderful bread. We can have sandwiches."

An hour or so later, armed with sunscreen, cold beer for the adults (with the exception of Lindsay, who was sticking to juice and water these days), and various toys and snacks to amuse Jack, the two younger couples and I found ourselves in lawn chairs in a shady part of the backyard. Catherine and Peter had made good on their promise to take Alexandra swimming.

"So Mom tells me that Uncle Charles is giving you life insurance lessons," said Andrew to Lindsay. "He's not bad, is he?"

"No, it's been great actually," said Lindsay.

Then the penny dropped.

"Hey, wait a sec. You mean you and Rebecca have also been schooled in the fine art of insurance? Uncle Charles, you do get around!"

Andrew grinned. "Well, not to the same extent as you and Daniel. Our education was limited to a few phone calls with Uncle Charles and a book or two on general financial planning."

"It's funny, Lindsay," I remarked, "just before Alexandra was born, Andrew and Rebecca and I had a conversation about life insurance similar to the one that you and Daniel and I have been having. My goodness, it must have been nearly eight years ago by now. This is déjà-vu. Refresh me, Rebecca — what did the two of you end up doing?"

"We got two ten-year term policies," said Rebecca, who had managed to slather a sufficient amount of sunscreen on a squirming Jack to let him get to his exploits in the sandbox. "And we also started RESPs for each of the kids after they were born. I remember, Charles, you said that registered education savings plans were like a form of insurance — insuring our children's future education by saving for it now."

"And the same thing with RRSPs — insuring our own retirement future," chimed in Andrew. "We're contributing the maximum each year, but that's not that much; neither of us has a lot of contribution room because of our pension plans at work."

"RRSPs and RESPs are a form of life insurance?" asked Lindsay. "I didn't know that."

"Technically, Lindsay, they are not forms of life insurance," I said. "So it's important not to confuse the two. But, to my mind at least, RRSPs and RESPs perform a function similar to life insurance: they help insure against financial hardship and preserve standard of living."

"How so?" asked Daniel.

"It's quite simple, actually, when you look at the bigger picture," I said. "You want to make sure that your children can go to university if they want to, correct?"

All four of my listeners nodded.

"Education's definitely a priority," said Lindsay.

"Well, a post-secondary education costs a lot of money. And by the time your kids are ready for it, it's going to cost a lot more. Therefore, you make sure that you start saving for their university education now, through RESPs — those are registered education savings plans — and other savings. In the same way you pay your insurance premiums, you contribute a small — or not-so-small, if you can afford it — amount every month to your child's RESP, starting, if possible, when that child is very young. Over the years, the amount of money grows, both through your regular deposits and through interest and investment earnings. What's more, you don't pay tax on the money that money earns until the funds are withdrawn. When your child goes to college or university, he or she pays for it with the money in the RESP. At that point, he or she will pay tax on that money. But because a student typically doesn't make much money, the tax rate is very low. You can put up to $4,000 a year into RESPs."

"The other great thing we found out is that the government will contribute to your kid's RESP," said Andrew. "They'll add 20 percent to the contribution you make each year, up to $400 a year for each kid."

"That's like free money," said Daniel.

"It *is* free money," said Andrew. "So if you put in $2,000 a year, you're actually getting $2,400, and that's before the money grows or earns any other interest."

"Interesting," quipped Lindsay.

"It is, very," I said. "A guaranteed return of at least 20 percent in the first year is great, and it's an opportunity that parents — and grandparents — should take full advantage of, in my opinion. The only catch is that the child *must* go to college or university in the end. Otherwise, that 20 percent will get clawed back."

"It's funny that you mention grandparents," said Andrew. "Rebecca's parents are making the RESP contributions for the kids. They put in fifty dollars a month each for Alex and Jack. They say they'd rather make sure that their grandchildren have a first-class education than fancy birthday presents or a big inheritance."

"I know many grandparents who feel the same way," I said. "Did you ever calculate just how much that fifty dollars a month will grow to by the time a child is eighteen years old? If the money, plus the government's contribution, earns an average of, let's say, 8 percent interest for eighteen years, you're looking at nearly $30,000."

"That would have taken a big chunk out of our student loans, Daniel," said Lindsay.

"No kidding," said Daniel. "So RESPs, like life insurance, are a way of making sure you'll have the necessary money for future expenses."

"That's right," I said. "And so are RRSPs. In addition to making sure that your kids get educated so that they can get good jobs and eventually move out of your house, you want to make sure that you can afford to retire and actually enjoy your empty nest. Therefore, you contribute to a pension plan, if you have one, through work, and to an RRSP — that's a registered *retirement* savings plan — so that you'll have an income post-retirement."

"Refresh me on the basics of RRSPs," said Daniel. "I know that you can contribute a certain amount of your income, up to a limit, and that that amount gets deducted from your total income, so you don't pay tax on it."

"Oh, you pay tax on it," I corrected him. "Governments get very edgy when you start talking about not paying taxes. You *defer* taxes — that is, you put money into the plan, where it grows, tax-sheltered, and you pay tax on it only when you withdraw it, usually in retirement. Often, however, you're in a lower tax bracket when you retire than you were when you were working full time, so you'll pay less tax on the money in retirement."

"You can put in up to 18 percent of your previous year's income, Daniel, or $13,500, whichever is less," added Rebecca.

"Yes, and that number will rise to $14,500 in 2004 and $15,500 in 2005," I added. "But because all you folks contribute to pension plans through work, your RRSP limits are lower. The government will adjust them to reflect your pension contributions, and your human-resources department — incidentally, the place you'll go, Lindsay and Daniel, to find out about your union's life insurance rates — can tell you what your adjusted RRSP contribution rates are. Or you can look on last year's T4 slip."

"That's what we do," said Andrew.

"We could talk all day about the ins and outs of RRSPs and RESPs," I said, "but frankly, there's a lot of great information out there already, including stuff on the Internet. My main point is that they, along with life insurance, are crucial parts of your financial planning. To my way of thinking, they serve the function of insuring your future. By the way, so do wills. If you have a will, you ensure that your estate gets divided up the way you want it to, and that your assets go to the people you want them to go to. If you die without a will, then the government will take care of that for you, which is not necessarily what you would have wanted. So add drawing up a will to your list of financial-planning activities that insure your future — and that of your dependants."

"So, Andrew," said Lindsay to her older brother, "you and Rebecca have wills, life insurance, two RESPs, *and* RRSPs? And pension plans at work?"

"Yeah," said Andrew. "And a mortgage. I guess it sounds a little overwhelming, but it was all pretty simple to set up, and now all the payments go like clockwork. Rebecca's parents take care of the RESPs. The RRSP contributions, the insurance premiums, and the mortgage payments come out of our bank accounts every month — well, the mortgage actually goes weekly. We never see the money, so we don't miss it. There's not a ton of cash left over, but it's enough to cover our other expenses."

"Barely," said Rebecca, with a wry grin. "Actually, we did one other thing, and that's probably the smartest investment we've made. We put a hundred dollars into a mutual fund each month — another investment that just comes right out of our chequing account. We started that as a 'rainy day' kind of account right after Alex was born, and there's more than $14,000 in there now."

"Wow," said Daniel.

"Wow is right," I agreed. "That's the value of compounding for you."

"Okay, Uncle Charles," said Lindsay. "As usual, I'll bite. What's compounding?"

"Put simply, it's earning interest on the interest your money earns. So if you invest $100 and earn 8 percent on it, and reinvest that eight dollars, the next year you'd earn interest on $108, if the interest is compounded annually.

And so on. That's how your RRSPs and RESPs will grow as well. Listen, if you want to know more details about the things we've been talking about — like wills, registered savings plans, saving money every month, mortgages — I'd suggest you read David Chilton's *The Wealthy Barber*. It's a great book on financial planning for beginners. It explains RRSPs and the like in detail, and it talks about the 'magic' of compound interest and why it's so valuable in terms of building wealth. The title character is a barber who's also a millionaire because he put away 10 percent of his income over the course of his working life. There's even a basic chapter on life insurance in there. And believe it or not, it's a fun read."

"We read that book, Lindsay," said Andrew to his little sister, "and we learned some important concepts from it. That's where we got the idea to put away the hundred bucks a month. It's not 10 percent of our income, but it's a start."

"Geez," said Lindsay. "If a barber can be a millionaire, how hard could it be for two teachers?"

"Two future principals," Daniel corrected her.

"I hate to tell the two of you this," said Andrew, "but a million bucks doesn't go as far as it used to these days." He stretched back on his lawn chair, a world-weary look on his face. Lindsay rolled her eyes, and Rebecca burst out laughing. Jack looked up from his sandcastle, startled.

"Don't worry, honey," said Rebecca. "Daddy's just being silly."

"Much as I hate to admit it, Andrew's right," I said. "Today, with inflation, not to mention taxes, a million dollars can get whittled away before you know it. The two of you are doing a great job of financial planning, Andrew and Rebecca. But I have a few suggestions for how you can get even more out of your investments."

"Really?"

"Yes. And now's probably a good time to discuss this,

because your ten-year term policies are coming up for renewal in a couple of years, so you'll want to look at your options for renewal then. There's a life insurance product that might make a lot of sense for you at this stage in your lives. It's called universal life."

"That's the product you told us we might want to look at after our ten-year term policies expired," said Lindsay.

"Correct," I said.

"What is it?" asked Andrew.

"Well, do you remember the bit of advice I gave all of you when you first thought about buying life insurance and didn't know what kind to buy?"

"Buy term?" asked Lindsay, after a pause.

"That's half the equation," I answered. "I suggested that you 'buy term and invest the difference.' That, essentially, is what Andrew and Rebecca have been doing until now, because they bought term policies and are putting away a hundred dollars a month. Well, universal life is like buying term and investing the difference, only you do it within the same insurance policy."

"That sounds like permanent insurance," said Daniel, puzzled. "What's the difference?"

"Well, universal life is a form of permanent insurance," I answered. "Actually, it's a combination of the best features of term *and* permanent insurance. It's more flexible than either of those products, though, and it has the added advantages of a tax shelter and a potentially lucrative investment."

"How does it work?" asked Rebecca.

"Well, universal life is essentially a term-to-100 insurance policy with a tax-advantaged investment portfolio tacked onto it. That does sound a bit like a whole-life policy, Daniel. But the similarities end there. First, unlike the investments offered by traditional permanent policies, which tend to be limited and conservative, with universal life you have more choice and control over where and how your money is invested. And with that increased choice and control comes the possibility for much higher returns, depending on the markets. You could invest in conservative GICs — those are guaranteed investment certificates issued by financial institutions — or in index funds that follow the stock exchanges — like the Toronto Stock Exchange or the Standard & Poor's 500. Or you could do a mixture of investments: put 25 percent in bonds, another 25 percent in international equities, another quarter in American equities, and the remainder in Canadian small-cap funds, if you'd like. It's up to you."

"So if the investments you have do well, you can make a lot more money than you could in a whole-life policy," said Lindsay.

"Yes," I said, "although the flip side is that with the increased choice and control, you also assume greater risk. If you invested everything in a NASDAQ-based index fund, for example, you wouldn't have done very well in March of 2000 — or since, for that matter."

"Uncle Charles, with traditional permanent policies, you said that either we could cash in the policy and get the built-up cash value or our beneficiaries could get the death benefit if we died," said Lindsay, who had obviously assumed a pretty powerful understanding of the ins and outs of the policies. "But you couldn't necessarily get both. Is there the same either/or with universal life?"

"No," I answered. "With universal life, or UL, your beneficiaries could receive both the death benefit *and* the built-up cash value in the policy if you died. As well, they'd receive it tax-free, and the money would bypass probate. What's more, you can withdraw cash that you've built up without having to cancel the policy."

"That sounds a lot better than traditional permanent insurance," remarked Daniel. "Why would people buy whole life when they could buy universal?"

"Well," I answered, "lots of people are asking the same

question. These days, more than half of new life insurance policies are UL accounts. Universal life has actually been around for a while, but it's increased in popularity in recent years. The insurance companies needed a product that could compete with the high interest rates of the 1980s and the boom markets of the 1990s, as well as with all the discount and on-line insurance products that have appeared in recent years. So they began to find ways to make life insurance more lucrative and attractive to investors."

"And they found it with this UL," said Andrew.

"Exactly," I said. "Now, Andrew, Rebecca, take that $14,000 you two have in your mutual fund. Every year, you've paid taxes on the money you've made from that investment. If you could defer or minimize the taxes, you'd have a lot more money to show for yourselves."

"So how do you defer taxes?" asked Andrew.

"Well, the most obvious way, which you've taken care of, is to maximize your RRSP contributions. You aren't taxed on the money you put into them, or the money they generate. Then, of course, there are your RESPs. You still pay for those with after-tax dollars, but the money they earn is tax-deferred. After that, one way to defer or minimize taxes is to invest that money in a universal life plan. Inside the plan, it would grow, tax-sheltered, up to a certain limit."

"Hold on," said Rebecca. "I'm not following."

"You know," I said, "I know exactly how to explain this to you all." I stood up. "Let's take a field trip."

"Where are we going?" asked Daniel.

"The tool shed," I said. "Follow me."

Andrew scooped Jack onto his shoulders, and we trooped over to the shed, which was at least as old as the cottage itself. In fact, Catherine suspected that it might have been the original building on the property, before the cottage and the guesthouse had been built. Now it housed gardening tools, lifejackets, and other odds and ends that no one knew what to do with but didn't want to throw away. I was hoping that one of those odds and ends was still there.

"Eureka!" I said after a few minutes of rummaging around like a madman. "I've found it!" I added unnecessarily.

I held up my treasure for my nieces and nephews to behold.

"Uncles Charles," said Andrew, "that's a rusty bucket with a hole in the bottom."

"It's like that song," chimed in Lindsay. "You know . . . 'There's a hole in the bucket, dear Charles, dear Charles . . .'"

"That's what makes it perfect," I said. "Listen, I'm going to use this leaky bucket to explain the basics of universal life insurance to you."

They looked doubtful.

"Trust me," I said.

We walked back towards the main cottage building, and around the side of the house, where the garden hose lay coiled on the ground. I turned on the hose so that only a trickle of water appeared.

"All right," I said. "Rebecca, this bucket is your new $100,000 universal life insurance policy. Congratulations."

"Thank you," she said.

I put the bucket on the picnic table and the hose into the bucket. The trickle of water leaked right out of the bottom of the bucket and was absorbed by the ground. A minuscule amount remained inside.

"Now," I told my pupils, "this empty bucket alone is worth, as I just said, $100,000 in death benefits. If you die, you get that money — as long as you've paid the premiums, that is. But those premiums are very flexible. You have both a minimum amount that you must put into the plan and a maximum amount that you can put in before the investment loses its tax-free status. And you can put in any amount in between.

"This trickle of water is the minimum payment," I continued. "With it, you're *minimum-funding* your policy, or covering only your costs: what it costs to insure you, the insurance company's expenses, taxes on insurance, and the sales agent's commissions. You've got your life insurance" — I thumped the bucket — "but very little else. Almost all the money you put in goes back out of the policy and to the insurance company to cover issue costs, just like this trickle of water runs right out the bottom of the policy — I mean, bucket. At this rate, you're not going to accumulate anything much inside the bucket, but you'll still have the policy. Does this remind you of anything?"

"That sounds like term insurance," said Lindsay. "No cash value, just pure insurance."

"Correct," I said. "When you minimum-fund the policy, you're essentially buying term insurance. But now, watch what happens when I turn up the water pressure."

I turned the faucet so that the trickle became an even flow. Water still leaked out of the bottom of the bucket, but now the level also began to rise inside.

"Now you're paying more than the minimum premium, or *overfunding* the policy," I said. "And so you begin to accumulate something inside your bucket, or universal life policy. You're still paying the costs of insurance, but you're also building up some equity, or savings."

A light came on in Rebecca's eyes. "Oh, I get it now, Charles! And those savings grow tax-free inside the bucket — or the policy," she said.

"Exactly," I replied. "Whatever extra you put into the policy beyond the cost of insurance will grow tax-sheltered until you take it out. To a point."

I turned the water on full blast. The bucket quickly filled up to the top and water began to run over the sides. Jack clapped his hands.

"Now, the bucket, obviously, can hold only a certain amount before it'll fill up completely and run over. The same holds true with universal life policies. There's a maximum amount of money — the technical term is the MTAR, or maximum taxable actuarial reserve — you can put into them before the government has a look and says, 'Hey, that's not really life insurance any more — that's a taxable investment!' Anything over that maximum amount will be taxed, just like any other investment."

"Oh," said Lindsay. "So what happens to the extra money? Where does it go?"

"Well, if you can afford to put in even more than your maximum, it would go into a side account. Jack," I said to my great-nephew, "can you get me a pail from the sandbox?"

Jack ran over to the sandbox and grabbed a yellow plastic pail. He returned and handed it to me solemnly.

"Thank you," I said. He high-fived me. I directed the overflowing water into the pail. "Here's your side account: a smaller bucket, so to speak, that is *not* exempt from taxation. If there's money in that account, you'll get a T5 form from the insurance company at the end of the year, and you'll have to pay tax on any interest or capital gains it generates. Or you can use some amount of that overflow to buy more insurance — essentially, a bigger bucket that'll hold more."

I turned off the water. We all watched as the bucket slowly emptied.

"And of course, if you stopped paying the premiums, the bucket might eventually empty, like this bucket here. What's more likely to happen, though, if you hold onto the policy long enough, is that it would eventually become self-funding — that is, the interest or investment income that the cash value generates would cover the costs of the premiums. Do you all understand the basics of universal life now?"

Everyone nodded — except for Jack, who had returned to the sandbox with the small yellow pail.

"Now, this is where it all gets interesting," I said as we strolled back towards our garden chairs and sat down. "Let's talk about that hundred dollars a month that Andrew and Rebecca are putting into mutual funds. First of all, I absolutely commend you for setting up that savings plan. I think it's one of the smartest things you could be doing with your money, and one day you're going to have a lot to show for it. But I'm hoping to show you how you can get even more out of that investment with universal life. Since your two ten-year term policies will be up in a couple of years, it might be a logical time to consider switching over to a universal life policy and putting your hundred dollars a month into that instead."

"What's the advantage?" asked Rebecca.

"Well, the first advantage is the one we've just discussed: tax savings. Right now, you're paying tax each year on the interest, dividends, and realized capital gains you've earned on the mutual fund. But when your money grows inside a universal life plan, you don't have to pay tax on your investment earnings until you withdraw them from the plan. The money grows sheltered from taxes, aside from provincial taxes on life insurance premiums, which range from 2 to 4 percent, depending on the province in which you live. So the first advantage is simple: you defer paying tax, possibly forever, on the money in your UL plan."

"That's smart," said Rebecca.

"It is," I agreed. "But it gets smarter. Let's take a look at the tax implications upon death. Lindsay and Daniel, let's see how much you remember from our earlier discussions. If you die, how much tax does the beneficiary of your life insurance have to pay on the death benefit?"

"None," they said in unison.

"The death benefit is tax-free *and* creditor-proof," added Daniel, laughing.

"Exactly. Okay, you've passed the pop quiz. Now, question two: Andrew and Rebecca, what happens when you two leave the contents of your mutual fund to your children?"

"They go on a big shopping spree," said Rebecca.

"Quite likely," I said. "But only after the estate pays capital gains taxes on the inheritance. And those taxes will eat up a sizeable chunk of the value of the fund. But what happens when you save the same money inside a universal life policy and your children are the beneficiaries of that policy?"

"They don't pay taxes on it?" Rebecca's eyes narrowed as she began to follow my line of reasoning.

"Correct. Not only has the money grown tax-sheltered all these years, but it's then paid out as a tax-free death benefit. It's a double whammy, in your favour, or rather, in favour of your beneficiaries. So say you have a policy for half a million dollars on your lives. And over the years, you've built up a considerable amount in the policy in cash value — say, another quarter of a million dollars, which, as we know from the 'magic' value of compound interest, isn't an unreasonable figure. That cash value has grown tax-free inside the policy. If you die without withdrawing it, your beneficiaries will receive the entire $750,000 as a death benefit. No taxes."

"That's incredible!" Andrew looked as though he had just hit pay dirt.

"It is pretty great," I said.

"I agree, Charles," said Rebecca, "And I can see that universal life would be a great way to give your beneficiaries a lot of money, tax-free. But what if you want to use the money you've saved while you're still alive? Andrew and I are putting away that hundred bucks a month for *us*, so that we can kick back and enjoy once the kids have grown up. We're not so worried about leaving a big inheritance."

"Very good point, Rebecca," I said. "And that's the really beautiful thing about universal life policies. Now, let's say that in twenty-five or thirty years, you and Andrew decide it's high time you spent some of that hard-earned cash you've been saving all these years. But when you go to withdraw, or surrender, say, $150,000 from the policy, what happens?"

"We get hit with a big tax bill," said Andrew, rubbing his forehead.

"That's right," I said. "If you want to get technical, you'll pay tax on the difference between the surrender value of the policy — which is the cash you've built up inside it — minus what's known as its ACB, or adjusted cost base. The ACB is used by the government to evaluate whether tax is payable on withdrawals or surrenders from the policy."

I looked at my pupils. They all had blank expressions on their faces.

"Okay, that was too technical," I admitted. "Just remember that you'll have to take the ACB into account in twenty or thirty or so years, when you're looking at the tax implications of cashing in your policy. More important in terms of our discussion, though, are the tax implications of withdrawing money from the plan. ACBs, surrender values, and the like aside, you could be faced with a hefty tax bill when you withdraw money from the plan in later years. So that option all of a sudden is a bit less attractive."

"Uh-huh," said Andrew.

"But what if you went to the bank and said, 'I've got a universal life insurance policy with a built-up cash value of $250,000. Can you give me a loan with that cash value as collateral?'"

"Will the bank say yes?" asked Rebecca.

"Yes, it generally will. Many insurance companies actually have agreements with banks to cover exactly that situation. So instead of withdrawing $250,000 from the policy and paying the taxes on it, you take a $250,000 loan with the policy as collateral, and pay, say, 8 percent interest or whatever the going rate is. Well, 8 percent of $250,000 is a lot less than the potential tax hit!"

"Oh! I get it!" said Andrew. "You live off the loan in your retirement, and when you die, the bank gets the money in the insurance policy to pay off the loan!"

"Bingo," I said. "And your beneficiaries get the death benefit. As long as interest rates are lower than your tax rate, you're doing well."

"That's brilliant, Charles!" said Rebecca. "When our ten-year term is up in the next couple of years, it looks like Andrew and I should convert to universal life."

"You don't have to wait until the term is up," I said. "I'm not suggesting that you rush into anything, but if you decide to convert your term policy to a UL one, the insurance company will let you do it whenever you want."

"Oh, okay," said Rebecca. "I guess I thought the term was binding."

"Nope," I said. "Have a look at universal life. I have to say it's an amazing product if you're the right type of investor. And I think you two are. You might also just consider diverting your hundred dollars a month from the mutual fund into the universal life plan. If you can achieve close to the same return on the funds you invest inside the plan as you can with your mutual fund, the tax-sheltering aspects of the UL account would make it the more lucrative investment. I would check it out. You know how *The Wealthy Barber* suggests saving 10 percent of your money in a mutual fund? In some ways, I think that saving 10 percent of your income inside a UL fund might just be the next logical step in that line of reasoning."

"But, Uncle Charles," asked Lindsay, "if universal life is so great, and if you should be saving 10 percent of your income anyway, why did you just spend all this time explaining to me and Daniel that our best choice is term insurance?"

"Good question," I answered. "But I have a good answer for you. There's no doubt that universal life is a great product. Let's recap its advantages. It offers life insurance, which you all need at the moment. It offers you investments that are potentially much more lucrative than those offered by traditional whole-life policies, and it gives you more control over those investments. It takes the mystery out of permanent insurance by 'unbundling' the product, so that you can easily see how much your insurance costs versus what you're investing. You couldn't do that with whole life, either. Maybe most important, it offers you tax advantages: as we've discussed, up to a limit determined by the government, the money you invest in these plans grows tax-free until you withdraw it. And in twenty-five or thirty years, it might just provide some retirement income for you, again at a very low tax rate. That, in my opinion, is its chief advantage.

"Having said all that, universal life isn't for everyone. And at this moment, I don't think that you and Daniel are the right type of investors for the product, though I think you could be in a while, as your circumstances change."

"Fair enough, but why?" asked Daniel.

"Well, let's compare term and UL. The first advantage of universal life is that it offers life insurance. Well, your life insurance needs are covered by the term policies you're about to buy, and you know you're getting all the insurance you need at low rates. As for unbundling the product, you know what you're getting with term insurance: life insurance, plain and simple. No mystery there.

"Third, and most important, universal life offers a tax shelter. But the two of you already have two tax shelters that you're not taking advantage of fully — your RRSPs and the RESP you'll contribute to for your child, or children. Why seek out yet another tax shelter until you've investigated the tax advantages in these two plans?"

"So we should work towards maxing out our RRSPs?" Daniel asked.

"Exactly. From what you tell me, both of you have out-standing room in your RRSPs. Contributing to those plans every year will net you a healthy tax savings and a shelter. Surprisingly, only about 10 percent of Canadians have contributed the full amounts to their RRSPs. In my opinion, that should be your first priority. And hey, if you get a tax refund from contributing to your RRSP, maybe you could invest that in the UL policy!"

"What about the RESP?" asked Lindsay. "Wouldn't that be our second priority?"

"Well, that's up to you, but since we've just discussed the fact that your children's education is important to you, you'll want to start saving for it now, because it won't be cheap. As we've discussed, tax is deferred on the money earned inside the plan. There's your tax shelter right there. Actually, it's a double shelter, because the funds will be taxed in the name of your child, who will likely have a very low tax rate. Plus, you're guaranteed a 20 percent first-year return on the first $2,000 you put into the plan each year because of the government's contribution. So you'll probably want to devote a portion of your investment money to the education of that baby" — I pointed at Lindsay's stomach — "and that may well take priority over coming up with the funds to invest in a UL policy."

"I see your point, Charles," said Daniel. "But you've just said that our pension plans will limit our RRSP room. And you can only put up to $4,000 a year into RESPs. So it might not take too much effort to put the maximum into our retirement plans. And maybe my parents would be willing to contribute towards our kids' education. Then wouldn't universal life become a definite possibility?"

"It might," I said. "Everyone's situation is different. You need to take a look at the bigger financial picture. For example, one of the most important factors in becoming wealthy is paying down debt, like your student loans and your mortgage — or credit cards! Someone who's paying 18 percent interest on a massive credit card debt, for example, would be well advised to pay off that debt before devoting cash to other non-essential investments. I'm not saying that only the debt-free should invest in universal life, but you'd have to weigh the financial pros and cons of carrying debt versus investing in UL and come up with a plan that works best for you. For example, if you can afford to, I would suggest that you double up your mortgage payments wherever possible and pay weekly or bi-weekly, to reduce the time you'll be paying off the mortgage. As well, pay back your student loans, and any other debts you have — *especially* credit card debts, which have an exorbitant interest rate. And then figure out if universal life fits into your strategy. From our discussion, Andrew and Rebecca are in a great position to contribute to a universal life policy: they've maximized their RRSP contributions, have taken advantage of the RESPs, pay their mortgage weekly, and have some money left over to invest each month."

"But couldn't we just open the universal life plan and contribute the minimum amount to it?" asked Lindsay. "You know, just have that trickle of water that runs right back out of the bucket?"

"That's a good question," I replied, "and yes, a lot of people do just that. But it's not a good idea because of something called the anti-dump-in rule."

"Great name," said Andrew.

"It's classy, isn't it? But it's exactly what it sounds like: a way of preventing people from doing what you just proposed, Lindsay. It's designed to make sure that people don't minimum-fund their universal life policies in the early years, and then all of a sudden begin to dump huge amounts into the policy in the later years."

"Why doesn't the government want you to do that?" asked Rebecca.

"Well, these plans are supposed to be primarily about life insurance. But they do have very generous tax-sheltering benefits. I guess the government is wary of people using UL plans only, or primarily, as a way of deferring taxes. So they've set up a few regulations, like the MTAR and the anti-dump-in rule, to make sure that people aren't simply using these plans to get out of paying tax."

"That's fair enough, I guess," said Daniel.

"I agree," I said. "The rule works like this: beginning in the tenth year of the policy, its value can't be more than 250 percent of what it was three years earlier. This is also known as the 250 percent rule. Not too many people know about it, but it could make a crucial difference to the value of your policy. That's why it's important, Lindsay, to contribute more than the minimum."

"I'm not sure I get how it works, though," said Daniel.

"Let's take an example. Say you and Lindsay decided to buy a universal life policy with a death benefit of $270,000. And let's say that the minimum contribution to the plan — that small trickle of water — is $1,500 a year and the maximum is $8,000. Because you've just bought a house, are contributing like mad to your RRSPs and your baby's RESP, and are living on a reduced income while Lindsay's on maternity leave, you decide to minimum-fund the policy for seven years, until you have a bit more financial breathing room — when your child will be in school full time, and you'll both be working full time too."

"Like me and Rebecca now that Jack's in preschool and daycare," chimed in Andrew.

"Exactly. So for the first seven years, you've put in the minimum amount of $1,500 each year. At the end of seven years, how much money have you built up in your account?"

"Well," said Rebecca, "you wouldn't have very much in it at all, because all the money's gone to cover the costs of your insurance. It's trickled right out the bottom of the bucket."

"Right. There would be only a very small amount built up. Remember, you've just been paying to cover the costs for what is essentially the term insurance you need, plus a small amount extra. Now, in year eight, you have a bit more money, and so you decide to put in an extra $1,000 or so a year to the policy — now you're overfunding, as opposed to minimum-funding. Then, in year ten, you both get promoted to principal, have paid off all your loans, and have even more money to contribute. So you decide that now would be a good time to contribute the maximum amount — the full $8,000 — every year. But the insurance company says, 'Hey, wait! You can't do that!' And then you remember the anti-dump-in rule! Because you put in only the minimum amount for the first seven years, your cash accumulation in year seven was worth very little, let's say $1,000, if that. And the rule states that beginning in year ten, the value of the policy can't be more than two and a half times what it was three years earlier. Two and a half times $1,000 is $2,500. So even though you have $8,000 to contribute, the most you can put in is $1,500, which would give you a value of $2,500."

"I get it now," said Daniel. "So if you wanted to use the policy as a tax shelter later on in life, the 250 percent rule limits the amount you can put in —"

"Unless you put in the maximum right from the start," finished Lindsay.

"Pretty much. It's very important not to minimum-fund the policy during the first seven years. I can't emphasize that enough with UL policies. On the other hand, you don't have to put in the absolute maximum every year, Lindsay, though if you could afford to, it would be a very nice investment. Actually, not many people put in the maximum. I used to tell my clients, and the agents who worked for me, that anyone purchasing a UL policy should deposit, at the very least, somewhere between 20 to 30 percent more than the minimum. With that amount of money going into the policy, you're in a position to take advantage of all its benefits.

"What it really comes down to is how much money you've got and how much you can afford to invest," I continued. "The bottom line is this: if you don't have a lot of debt or RRSP room, and can afford to invest in a universal life plan above and beyond your RRSPs, RESPs, basic term insurance costs, mortgages, and everything else that goes into the cost of living, do it. If you can afford to save 10 percent of your income on top of that, do that too. There are all kinds of options. You have to look at what you can afford to do."

"I wonder if we can," said Rebecca. "I mean, we're doing pretty well, but there doesn't seem to be any money just floating around at the end of each month after all the other obligations and investments are paid off. We're stretched pretty thin."

"Yeah," said Andrew. "There always seems to be something we hadn't counted on, like a new muffler for the car or replacing the oven."

"I understand," I said. "If you'd like, I can pull out my laptop and run a quote that would let you know how much a universal life policy would cost for each of you. We could look at the minimum and maximum premiums, and compare them with the costs of another set of ten-year term policies. But in the end, you have to do what's most comfortable for you, financially and emotionally."

"I like the idea of running a quote," said Rebecca.

I stood up. "I'll be back in a moment," I said as I went to retrieve my computer from my bedroom in the guest house. When I returned, my students were still talking animatedly.

"We were just talking about how great it is to have our own personal financial advisor, Uncle Charles," said Lindsay as I sat down again.

"I'm glad to be of service," I said as I turned on the notebook. The battery was fully charged, so I knew I'd be able to run a few quotations without finding an extension cord. As we waited for the little machine to power up, I continued the lesson on UL.

"There are a few other things you should know about universal life policies," I said. "The first is that like all other investments, they always carry risks. We've already talked about the fact that they have the potential for large gains, but there's nothing to say that your investments won't tank either. You have to choose wisely when it comes to the kinds of index funds you invest in for your UL policy.

"As well," I continued, "the investment funds inside universal life policies can sometimes have higher costs associated with them than index funds or similar investments outside a UL plan. Management expense ratios, MERs, can run a bit higher. That said, the tax savings will often outweigh those costs. It'll depend on how you invest the money.

"Another thing to take into account is that UL is a long-term financial strategy. It'll take fifteen or twenty years for the real benefits of the plan to become apparent, and you'll have to stick to the schedule of payments for that time. Now, you do have some flexibility in that schedule. You could, for example, pay more into the policy some years and less in other years. But remember the importance of investing as much as you can in the first seven years!"

"Got it," said Lindsay. "No minimum-funding the policy in the early years."

"The other thing to think about," I continued, smiling, "is the cost of insuring you. You can choose to go with a level cost of insurance, which will stay the same for the entire policy, kind of like premiums for permanent insurance. Or you can choose YRT — yearly renewable term — premiums."

"What's the difference?" asked Rebecca.

"Either way, your minimum and maximum premiums stay the same," I replied. "But with YRT, the amount of the premium that goes to cover the actual cost of insuring you varies according to your age. So in the early years, when it costs less to insure you against premature death, more of your money goes towards your investments. In the later years, when your risk of death is higher, more of the premium goes to life insurance coverage and less to the investments."

"What are the implications of choosing either one?" asked Andrew.

"There are pros and cons to each, depending on your goals," I said. "If your main goal is to accumulate and shelter as much money as possible, as quickly as possible, you'd probably choose YRT, because you'd have more money to invest in the early years, and that money would have more time to grow. It tends to work better the more money you have to invest. However, there will come a point when you're old enough that your insurance costs become *very* high. At that point, more of your premium is going towards life insurance coverage. The downside to YRT is that the increasing costs of insurance could erode the value of your investment."

"So if you wanted to know that your insurance costs would remain stable, you'd choose level premiums, right?" asked Daniel.

"Right. With level premiums, you're averaging out the cost of insurance over the life of the policy. You pay more in the early years and less in the later years. You invest less money at the beginning of the policy, but your costs don't go up."

"That's like the difference between term and permanent insurance, isn't it?" Lindsay remarked.

"It is," I replied. "And in the same way that many people choose term insurance in their early years of coverage and switch to permanent as they get older, many people start off with YRT, which makes sense until about middle age, and then they switch to level."

The notebook had booted up, and I opened my company software to run the insurance quotes. When Jack saw the computer, he came running over from the sandbox.

"Computer games!" he shouted, throwing himself into my lap. His parents began to laugh.

"No, honey," said Rebecca. "This isn't a computer game. Uncle Charles is helping Mommy and Daddy with math."

"But you can help me, Jack," I said. "You can find the numbers I need and punch them in."

The little boy nodded happily, and with a bit of effort on his part, we managed to enter in the information for Andrew, a thirty-five-year-old male, non-smoker, and Rebecca, thirty-three, also a non-smoker. First we checked out the cost for another ten-year term policy at $400,000. Then we ran the numbers for a universal life policy with the same amount of insurance coverage.

"Okay, here's the difference," I said. "The yearly premium for another ten years of term will be in the range of $440. For universal life, your minimum premium, assuming level premiums, is $1,860 a year and your maximum premium is almost $10,800. Rebecca, your rates are approximately $376 for term. Your minimum UL premium is $1,400 and your maximum is $9,000."

"Wow," said Rebecca. "I thought we were doing well with a hundred dollars a month. I can't imagine how we'd come up with $10,000."

"But you don't need to — do they, Uncle Charles?" Lindsay turned to me. "You can put in 20 to 30 percent more than the minimum and it's still useful, right?"

"Right," I answered. "So Andrew could be looking at an investment of between $2,200 and $2,400 a year, around $200 a month, for this to be a good product for you. And remember, your insurance costs are included in that price. With an annual premium of $2,400 a year, growing at, say, 8 percent a year, you'd have" — I punched the figures into my notebook — "about $155,000 cash value and $555,000 in total death benefits by the age of sixty-five. By the time you turned seventy, the cash value would be $260,000, and the death benefit would be close to $670,000."

"Wow," said Daniel.

"What does 'total death benefits' mean?" asked Rebecca.

"That's the cash value plus the death benefit — the total amount your beneficiaries would receive if you die."

"Hmmm," said Andrew to his wife, "we might just be able to afford it."

"If not now, then in a couple of years, when the term policies are up anyway," answered Rebecca. "I don't want to sacrifice our standard of living now, but I'm pretty impressed by the tax savings later on with universal life."

"It is definitely a plan with an eye for the future," I concurred. "You know who you might want to talk to about this? Your Aunt Joyce. She's a perfect example of someone who's made universal life work well. Give her a call."

My younger sister, Joyce, had certainly done well with universal life. She and her husband, Rob, would be up to the cottage in August. I'd get an update from her then.

"Mom! Dad! We saw fish! And I did a back flip off the diving board!"

Alexandra, wrapped in a towel, her hair streaming wet down her back, came running up from the direction of the lake. Peter and Catherine followed behind, as Alex settled in on Andrew's lap and grabbed a cookie and a juice box.

"What have you folks been up to?" asked Peter, helping himself to a cookie or two.

"Oh, the usual," said Lindsay. "Life insurance. We can't get enough of it."

"Well," I said, "I don't know about the rest of you, but I could use a swim. Andrew, Rebecca, those are pretty much the basics of universal life. If you have more questions, let me know. Alex, once you've had a rest, I want to see that back flip!"

RECIPES FOR SUCCESS

1   RRSPs, RESPs, and wills are all part of a sound financial plan. Like life insurance, they help to "insure" your own and your family's financial security. And like the money invested in universal life insurance products, the money invested in RRSPs and RESPs grows tax-deferred.

2   Universal life is a product that allows you to "buy term and invest the difference" — all within the same policy.

3   The cash accumulated inside a UL account grows tax-deferred (up to a point!), which allows for greater wealth accumulation than taxed investments.

4   Remember the 250 percent rule! It's important not to minimum-fund your universal life policy in the first seven years. Try to invest at least 20 to 30 percent above your minimum premium cost when the policy is young. Otherwise, you might find that the amount you can invest later is limited.

6

Life Insurance for the Living:

Disability Insurance, Critical Illness Insurance, and Living Benefits

"Peter, Charles, have you heard the car yet? They should have been back by now."

My sister-in-law walked onto the deck, where Peter and I were playing chess. Our father had taught us to play when we were children, and during most extended visits, Peter and I tended to engage in a little friendly sibling rivalry over the chessboard. His analytical mind made my brother a natural for the game. My years in the insurance business, on the other hand, had perhaps helped me sharpen my own chess skills: I'd made a career of envisioning and planning for a range of future scenarios, a skill I found quite handy when it came to deciding on the next move (or three). We were probably equally matched partners, although we would never admit it to each other.

Catherine usually left Peter and me alone when the chessboard came out. She said that there was nothing less entertaining than watching a pair of preoccupied old men stare at a game for hours, grunting or making cryptic comments. She was happier with novels and crosswords, and would occasionally take the time to beat the pants off both of us — and whoever else happened to be around — at Scrabble.

But today I detected a note of worry in my sister-in-law's voice. And I *had* noticed that Peter had been checking his watch for the past hour or so.

"When were they supposed to be back here?" I asked. Lindsay and Daniel had left for Ottawa that morning to meet my niece Karin at the airport. She'd taken the red-eye from Vancouver, via Toronto, and they — rather cheerfully, in my opinion — had offered to get up early to meet her at 8:10 a.m. Now, it was nearly noon.

"Even with the rush-hour traffic, I expected them a good hour ago," said Catherine. "I know they called to make sure the flight was on time."

"Well," I offered, "I wouldn't worry yet. Traffic could be bad, or they might have decided to stop for breakfast."

At that moment, as if on cue, we heard the sound Catherine and Peter had been listening for all morning — a car turning onto the road at the front of the cottage property. Seconds later, Lindsay and Daniel's car appeared. They waved as it rolled to a stop, and then they climbed out wearily. Karin emerged from the back seat, and her relieved parents and I moved excitedly down the walk to greet them.

"What happened?" asked Catherine.

"We crawled along for a good two hours," said Karin. "There was a nasty accident on the highway, and the police were diverting traffic. It was the last thing I needed after being on a plane all night. But I'm sorry you were worried."

My niece Karin is thirty-two. She's always had a flair for writing — editor of the high-school yearbook and her university's student newspaper. She moved out to Vancouver after earning a B.A. in communications to do an M.B.A. at the University of British Columbia. Now she's turned her skills into a thriving small business on the West Coast: after working for KPMG for a few years, she decided to become her own boss. She's a self-employed communications and marketing consultant for professional firms. She bought a two-bedroom condo (not, fortunately, one of the leaky ones that have plagued some Vancouver condo owners) last year, and works out of her fully equipped home office. Business, apparently, has been great; Catherine and Peter told me that Karin had wanted to spend more than just four or five days at the cottage, but she was too busy to take more time off.

Right now, however, she just looked tired.

"Come inside, all of you, and have some coffee," said Catherine. "And your Uncle Charles has made some of his world-famous cinnamon buns to go with it."

"Great!" said Lindsay. "I'm starving, as usual."

"Oh, yeah," said Karin, flashing me a smile as we walked into the kitchen and sat down at the table. "I've heard all about Uncle Charles: bread-making and life insurance seminars under the same roof!"

"Well, I do have to make myself useful," I joked. "You know, earn my keep."

"It's been amazing," said Lindsay, licking icing off her fingers. "The insurance lessons, too."

Daniel elbowed her gently. "But seriously," he said, "as we sat there in the car and listened to news reports about this fatal six-car pileup that was holding up traffic, I found myself feeling really glad to know what we now know about life insurance. It sounds macabre, but what if it had been me in that accident? Charles, when we get back to Ottawa, the first thing on our to-do list is to meet up with that insurance representative you mentioned and get our life insurance sorted out."

"Huh," said Karin. "Now I'm wishing I could've sat in on a few of those seminars. I really don't know a thing about life insurance."

"You don't need life insurance, though," said Lindsay, displaying her new-found wisdom. "You don't have any dependants, and your business is doing well enough that we shouldn't have to pay your debts after you're gone — I hope."

"What I'm most worried about isn't dying and debt," mused Karin. "My only debt is my condo, and that's covered by mortgage insurance. I'm more concerned about getting sick and not being able to work. I mean, I don't have any employee benefits, and I'm not covered by any kind of workers' compensation or government employment insurance. That's the biggest thing I miss about working for someone else: the benefits! You know, last year I had the flu for two weeks, and it took me nearly a month to catch up financially."

"You're right to be concerned about illness getting in the way of work, Karin," I said. "It's actually more of a risk to you than premature death. For example, did you know that a woman your age is about seven times more likely to be disabled before the age of sixty-five than she is to die prematurely?"

"Really?" My nieces and nephew-in-law looked at me, worried expressions on their faces.

"Yes. The stats aren't encouraging: a thirty-year-old has something like a 52 percent chance of being disabled for ninety days or more before the age of sixty-five. And if a disability lasts at least ninety days, statistics show that it's likely to last for three or more years, depending on your age. That's a long time to go without an income. Lindsay's right, Karin. You probably don't need life insurance. But it does sound like you could use some disability insurance."

Karin yawned over her cinnamon bun. "You know, what I could *really* use right now is a nap. I know I just got here, and I would love to sit down right away and visit — and talk to you more about disability insurance, Uncle Charles — but I think I'll be much better company once I've managed to get in a couple hours of sleep. In a bed, as opposed to an airplane seat."

Catherine checked into full mothering mode.

"Yes, sweetheart, you do need some rest. I've made up

your bedroom, and we can all catch up after you've had a nap."

"That sounds heavenly," said Karin. "Where's the bed?"

"And in the meantime," said Peter, "I will finish trouncing your Uncle Charles in our chess match."

"Not so fast," I said. "I have a few tricks up my sleeve yet."

◆ ◆ ◆

"So who won the chess game?" asked Karin, looking considerably brighter as she entered the living room a few hours later.

"Well, *I* would have won if —" Peter began good-naturedly as I started to protest that he had cheated.

"It was a draw," said Catherine, interrupting our bravado. "They almost always draw. They both use the same tricks, and they can never outsmart each other."

"Great minds think alike, I guess," I quipped. "How was your nap?"

"It was great," said Karin. "I feel like a new person. There's nothing like waking up and knowing you're on vacation."

We ate lunch on the deck and did some catching up — Karin had brought photos of a recent trip to Vancouver Island, and she filled us in on West Coast life.

"All the rumours about Vancouverites are true," she told us. "I've been completely converted. I'm a regular at Starbucks, and I rollerblade and snowboard all the time. And I eat tons of sushi. Lindsay, you and Daniel will have to come visit with the baby next summer."

"We'd love to," said Lindsay. "It's funny, though. I have no idea what our life will be like this time next year. Things are going to be so different with a baby in the picture. I really can't imagine how we'll make plans."

"Speaking of making plans," said Karin, "I wouldn't mind talking about that disability insurance, Uncle Charles. You've got me thinking about it. I think I might even have dreamt about it."

"Sure," I said. "Any time."

"Well, how about right now?" said my niece. "Does anyone mind?"

"Not at all," said Catherine. "I've been dying to sit in on one of Uncle Charles's insurance seminars, see what it is he's been telling you all."

"Me too," said Peter.

"I'm game," said Daniel. "You've got us curious about disability insurance now, too, Charles, and wondering if we need it."

"Well, all right then," I said, smiling. "Let's make this a family event."

"One second," said Karin. "Let me get a notebook and a pen!"

And so began the next session of Uncle Charles's Cottage-Country Life Insurance Seminars. I wondered if I should start printing up flyers.

"Karin," I began once my niece had returned, writing equipment in hand, "let me ask you a question: what's your most valuable asset?"

"That's easy," she said quickly. "My condo."

"Not so fast," I countered. "You might have invested a lot in your condo, but you have something else that's much more valuable."

"I do?" My niece looked at me through squinted eyes. "This is a trick question, isn't it?"

"Not at all," I said. "What would cause you the greatest financial hardship if you were to lose it?"

"Oh, okay! You mean my health, don't you?"

"Close. Specifically, I mean your ability to earn a living. Whatever you paid for your condo — even a condo in Vancouver! — probably doesn't come close to the amount of money you'll make over the course of your working life.

Since we've been throwing around statistics today, here are a
few more: a thirty-five-year-old who makes $3,000 a month
today will earn approximately $2.4 million by the age of
sixty-five, assuming her earnings increase by 5 percent a
year. If she earns $4,000 a month, her lifetime earnings will
be more like $3.2 million."

"Wow," said Lindsay.

"Wow is right. That's a lot of earnings at stake in the
event of a permanent disability. If you became ill, Karin, or
were injured in, say, a freak snowboarding accident, and
could no longer work, just imagine the financial hardship
that could cause."

"I wouldn't be able to make my mortgage payments,"
said Karin, "and the bank would foreclose."

"Good point. Disability accounts for more than half of all
mortgage foreclosures. You'd be out of a home. And what if
you had a partner or children, or both, who depended on
your income? They'd be out of a home, too, plus a whole lot
more."

"Yeah, like food and clothing. So I definitely need to buy
insurance against disability," said Karin.

"Not quite," I answered. "Even the best disability insurance policy in the world can't prevent you from injuring
yourself or becoming ill, just like the best life insurance
policy can't prevent you from dying. You buy disability insurance to protect your income in the event that you aren't able
to earn money. That's all disability insurance really is —
a way of protecting your current and future income."

"Well put," said my niece with a grin. "But I wouldn't even
know where to begin. I mean, how much do I need?"

"Well," I replied, "in the case of disability insurance, you
don't really have to figure out how much you *need*. Instead,
you have to figure out how much you *qualify for*, and that
amount is based on how much you earn right now. If you're
employed and have a group disability plan through your

work, the benefits usually cover between 66 and 70 percent of your salary before taxes."

"Is that what Lindsay and I have?" asked Daniel.

"Yes," I replied, "which is the reason I didn't suggest that you two rush out to buy disability insurance. Because you already have disability plans through your jobs, you'll probably find it difficult, if not impossible, to buy any more coverage. Also, because you contribute to the government's employment insurance, or EI, plan and to the Canada Pension Plan, you're eligible for some government disability benefits. There's also workers' compensation, if you work in an eligible industry and are injured on the job. You can even combine the benefits of all the plans you qualify for. But they will be co-ordinated and capped so that you end up with only that 66 percent or so of your salary."

"So," said Catherine, "if you don't have an income, you don't qualify for disability insurance, right?"

"That's right," I said. "In your case, Karin, because you're self-employed, you don't have any pre-existing group coverage through an employer, nor are you eligible for EI benefits, although you might be eligible for benefits under the Canada Pension Plan, if you've been contributing to it. But basically, if you become disabled, you're on your own! And therefore, you would have to buy a private disability plan. The benefit you qualify for would be based on an average of your earnings over the past few years."

"How do they find out how much I earned?" asked Karin.

"Insurance companies are very thorough about that," I answered. "You have to provide proof of income, usually your tax returns for the past couple of years."

"Why only two-thirds or so of your salary?" Catherine wanted to know.

"For two reasons. The first is that the payments are tax-free, provided you pay for the premiums with after-tax dollars. So essentially, you make up most of the deficit right there. The second reason is that the insurance company — or the government, if you have government disability benefits — wants you to have some incentive to get back to work. If you could collect disability benefits equal to your salary, you might not be so interested in going back to your job."

"So are disability plans sort of a one-size-fits-all deal, then?" asked Karin. "I mean, if the benefit amount is set."

"Not at all," I said. "Just as with life insurance, there are all kinds of plans and options, and choosing the right mix is crucial. For example, you can choose a shorter or longer elimination period. That's the amount of time you'll have to be disabled before the plan will start to pay out benefits. Usually, people choose one of thirty, sixty, or ninety days, although you can have a zero elimination period, which is the most expensive. You can also go up to 120 or 180 days, or even a year or more, although I don't know many folks who opt for the longer ones.

"Also, you can choose a shorter or longer benefit period, which is the maximum length of time that benefits will be paid out. That could be anywhere from two years up to the age of sixty-five, when you'll no longer qualify. And of course, the shorter the elimination period and the longer the benefit period, the more costly the plan."

"So," said Karin, "if you had enough savings to get by for three months, you could choose a ninety-day elimination period and save on premiums, right?"

"That's right," I replied. "It's a good strategy, as long as you take into account that your disability might cost a lot of money. Your savings might be enough to cover three months' worth of your expenses in good health. But what if you had to buy expensive medication or therapies, or needed to hire a caregiver for yourself or a babysitter for your children? What if you had to buy a wheelchair or retrofit your home? What if you had business expenses that still had to be paid, even if you weren't earning an income? All of a sudden, you've got expenses you hadn't counted on. When you're considering the elimination period, make sure you consider those extra potential costs, and weigh those against the cost of the premiums for a shorter elimination period."

"Charles," said Daniel, "what about the type of work you do? I mean, if Karin broke her ankle snowboarding, she might be able to work just fine, with a few adjustments. But say you worked in construction or as a ski instructor?"

"Or a gym teacher," interjected Lindsay.

"Or a gym teacher," repeated her husband. "What then?"

"Well, this is where you get into the grey areas of disability," I answered. "Obviously, an injury or illness will mean different things to different people. An ankle injury for a writer or an accountant is probably a painful annoyance, but not a threat to his or her ability to earn an income. For a construction worker, however, it's potentially devastating. Or think about this: one person might be able to work, more or less, through chemotherapy, while the same treatment could send someone else to bed for months. What the insurer will do is look at each case individually. If an injury or illness prevents someone from doing his or her job, then that person is usually considered to be disabled, and disability benefits will usually kick in. The final say on who's disabled, however, belongs to the insurance company, which will refer cases to doctors to determine whether a disability exists and its extent. So you have to read the provisions very carefully.

"And," I continued, "insurance companies take all these differences into account when they price disability insurance. As we just discussed, they'll look at the type of work you do, how specialized it is, how much it pays, and the risks it carries. If, like Karin, you work at what's mostly a desk job, it's likely that your risk of injury will be lower than that of someone who works in construction. Therefore, your premiums will be lower.

"Companies also base premium costs on the incentive

you have to return to a job," I continued. "Again, a construction worker, who does physically demanding, potentially
dangerous work, might not be so inclined to return to a
building site after a long illness. On the other hand, a white-
collar worker, or a professional like a doctor or lawyer, tends
to have more incentive and desire to return to his or her job.
I'm not suggesting here, by the way, that blue-collar workers
are lazy or less willing to work! But what *is* true is that blue-
collar jobs can be more physically demanding or dangerous
than desk jobs, and someone who's been sick or injured
once may not have the physical stamina — or the desire —
to get back into a factory or a building site, where the chance
of re-injury is higher. Also, people who work at physically
demanding jobs, unlike white-collar workers, will generally
need to recuperate completely before going back to work.
Often, disability contracts will contain provisions for rehabilitation to help people get back to work."

"Wouldn't stress figure into a person's desire to go back
to work?" asked Peter. "I mean, there are lots of incredibly
stressful so-called white-collar jobs out there. Air-traffic controllers come to mind. I can't imagine that an air-traffic
controller with a heart condition would be very eager to get
back to work either."

"Good point," I said. "Insurers take all kinds of factors
into account when assessing jobs. In fact, they use morbidity
tables to classify jobs according to a scale of most to least
insurable. Where your profession fits on that scale will
determine how much coverage you can get and for how
long — or even if you can get coverage at all. Doctors,
lawyers, accountants, and other professionals — like archi-
tects — are usually classed as '4A,' which means that they
should easily qualify for disability insurance, provided
they're in good health, and their benefits will usually go to
age sixty-five if the disability is permanent. Their risk of
injury is low and their motivation for getting back to work is

high. As a result, they're able to get more benefits and their costs will be lower. A 4A might pay sixty-five dollars per thousand dollars of monthly benefit, while a 3A or a 2A might pay eighty dollars."

"I *knew* I should have become a doctor," said Daniel, shaking his head.

"If you were choosing a career based on your ability to get disability insurance, then yes, you should have become a doctor," I said. "Fortunately, you chose a job you actually like! Where that job fits in terms of insurance categories is a different story, though. After 4A, there's '3A,' which would include people like advertising executives and bank managers — even the clergy fits into 3A! These people don't necessarily have professional degrees, but they do have a certain amount of education, expertise, and I suppose, authority, and their risk of injury isn't that high."

"So where do teachers fit in?" asked Lindsay.

"Teachers, I hate to tell you, fit in lower than you would think," I answered. "They're usually in class A — that is, below 4A, 3A, and 2A. There are a lot of stress-related disability claims from teachers. Anyway, what class A means is that there might be limits on the amount of private disability coverage you could get or on how long the benefits would last, or both. Bus drivers and mechanics are also As. High-school principals, however, are classed as 2A."

"That's grim," said Daniel. "I didn't realize I worked in such a dangerous profession!"

"Well, don't worry too much about it," I said. "You've probably already got disability insurance through your collective agreement, as well as the government employment insurance program, to cover you for short-term disabilities, so not qualifying for much private coverage shouldn't be such a big loss."

"If teachers have high disability rates, what about roofers or construction workers?" asked Karin. "I mean, they're at a lot more physical risk than Lindsay and Daniel," she pointed out.

"Not some days," said Lindsay, shaking her head. "Come by my gym class sometime. I'll show you physical risk — a bunch of eighth-graders with volleyballs."

"Point taken," I said, laughing. "But to answer your question, Karin, roofers and construction workers and the like are usually in class B or A, depending on the insurer's classification system. This means they'd qualify for limited benefits, or perhaps benefits for disabilities that didn't result from their jobs. Usually, the benefit period is either two or five years. So if a roofer was in a car accident unrelated to work, then maybe he — or she, for that matter — could get some disability benefits. And then there are those jobs that are filed under U, for uninsurable. Peter, that's where your air-traffic controllers fit in. There's just too high a rate of stress and burnout in that job to make it worthwhile for insurance companies to cover it. Actors, by the way, are also uninsurable — insurance companies don't want to underwrite disability insurance for a career that can be unstable. Again, however, people who fall into category U might just qualify for some coverage through their unions, so all is not lost."

"Uncle Charles," said Karin, "what about factors outside your job? I mean, what about your risk of developing an illness like cancer or multiple sclerosis? Or what if you smoke? Will your disability insurance cost more if you have a family history of disease or you're a smoker?"

"Whoa! One question at a time," I said. "I think what you're asking is whether other factors come into play when an insurance company decides if you're eligible for coverage and what kind. And the short answer is yes. In addition to a financial check to see how much you earn, the insurance company will ask questions about your family history of illness and your lifestyle. If you've got a strong family history of cancer or heart disease, your disability premiums might be slightly more expensive, your benefits might not last as long, or the insurance company might exclude coverage for the hereditary condition. And of course, if you have a pre-existing illness when you apply for the insurance, it won't cover a disability resulting from that condition."

"Wouldn't you have to have a medical exam before you got coverage anyway?" asked Karin.

"Sometimes," I replied. "You'll have to fill out a medical questionnaire when you apply for coverage. Depending on your answers and the amount you're applying for, the company might request a medical exam. You might need only height, weight, and blood-pressure tests. Or you could need a full physical, depending on your health, the amount of coverage you qualify for, and your job. Mostly, it depends on the amount of coverage per month you're applying for. The higher it is, the more likely you'll have to take a medical."

"What if you smoke?" asked Daniel.

"The company will also do a so-called lifestyle check to see if you smoke or have dangerous hobbies, like parachuting, bungee jumping, or scuba diving," I answered. "If you're a smoker, your premiums will be higher, as they might be if you have high-risk hobbies. In these cases, the insurance company might still issue you a disability policy, but it could specifically exclude a disability resulting from a dangerous sport or hobby. So a recreational pilot wouldn't be able to claim benefits for an injury resulting from a plane crash. Or you might not be eligible for coverage at all, depending on the insurance company and your personal profile. By the way, they'll also ask about drug and alcohol use, and your driving record."

"What about mental health?" asked Lindsay. "Can you collect disability benefits if you're depressed, or have schizophrenia or something?"

"Yes, unless your policy dictates otherwise, and some do," I replied. "Remember, for general purposes, a disability is defined as a condition that prevents you from being able to do work. So if you're severely depressed and can't work as a result of that depression, you should be able to collect benefits. Again, you'd have to see what the policy included. Some companies put limits on how long they'll cover you for depression or mental illness."

"What if you could work at *something*, but not necessarily your old job?" asked Daniel. "I mean, what if that construction worker couldn't build houses, but he could teach people how to build houses? Or do a different job altogether?"

"Good question," I said. "And again, it depends on the type of policy you buy. There are a few different types. If you buy an 'own occupation' policy, it will cover you if you can no longer work at . . . well, your own occupation. So if a surgeon develops a neurological disorder that leaves her with shaky hands and unable to do her job, she would receive disability benefits under an own-occupation policy, even if she could do other work in her field, like teaching or examining patients."

"That seems very specific," observed Peter.

"It is — own-occupation policies are usually aimed at specialists, like doctors or lawyers — those 4A folks. And they're very expensive. The most expensive 'own occ' policy will even let you collect benefits while you're working at a different job."

"What do non-specialists qualify for?" asked Catherine.

"Well, a 'regular occupation' policy covers you if you can't do work within your field or profession. So if our hypothetical surgeon had this type of policy, she wouldn't receive disability benefits because she'd still be able to teach, make diagnoses, and do other related work. Regular occupation offers the incentive to work within your field, but it wouldn't force you to do just any job, which is what an 'any occupation' policy is. For this type of policy, you'd have to be incapable of doing *any* job to qualify — at least, any job for which you're reasonably suited by education, training, or experience."

"What does *that* mean?" asked Karin.

"Well, that's the problem. The definition isn't crystal clear. It might mean that the insurance company decides you're reasonably experienced and trained well enough to be a telemarketer or a security guard, or to work a cash register."

"That's scary," said Karin. "I'd really want to stay within my field."

"I agree," I said. "You've worked very hard to get to where you are professionally. Why would you want to give that up? 'Any occupation' disability insurance is the least expensive coverage, but remember, you get what you pay for.

"Along the same lines, there are also plans that require you to be not only disabled, but *totally and permanently* disabled before you can collect benefits. Actually, the CPP and Quebec Pension Plan disability plans also require that you have a 'severe and prolonged' disability, which is essentially the same thing. Be careful with these, though: a disability that lasts a year could be a huge financial hardship even if it isn't permanent. As well, it might be difficult to judge whether a disability will last forever."

"Okay, so it sounds like I should look into own- or regular-occupation disability insurance," said Karin, writing the phrases in her notebook.

"Yes," I said, "but you should also know that after two years of disability, even a regular-occupation policy can be modified so that you would be required to work at any job for which you're reasonably qualified because of your education, training, or experience."

"In other words, it would turn into an any-occupation plan," said Peter.

"Yes, essentially," I said. "Or you could say that the definition of 'disability' changes after two years, from not being able to do *your* job to not being able to do *any* job in your field. The insurer has a lot invested in the possibility that you will be able to return to work eventually, and it will require you to report in periodically on your condition. You'd have to check the provisions of the policy to see what it requires."

"What if you could work part time?" asked Catherine. "Or what if you had a disease or an injury that affected your ability to work, but over a long period of time? I mean, look at all these illnesses out there, like chronic fatigue syndrome or multiple sclerosis, that progress so slowly. Is there a policy that covers those?"

"Well, lots of disability plans have partial or residual disability features that either come with the policy or can be added on as riders. These will pay some of your benefits while you work part time, perhaps as a disease progresses. It makes sense, really: if you *can* work part time, it's in the best interest of the insurance company to let you, because they have to pay fewer benefits. It's also in your best interest, generally, to take advantage of the opportunity to get out in the world and be productive. So someone with chronic fatigue or MS could continue to work even after his or her diagnosis, cutting back only as the disease progressed. The residual disability feature is a good one because it means that you don't have to be completely disabled to collect benefits."

"Uncle Charles," said Lindsay, "can you buy term or permanent disability insurance, like you can with life insurance?"

"Not really," I replied, "but there are some similarities. Instead of choosing the term, you'd choose a benefit period, which can range anywhere from two years to age sixty-five, as we discussed. And of course, sometimes the term chooses you, depending on your job classification. Even if you want benefits paid up until you're age sixty-five, you might not be able to get it if you're an A or a B, for example.

"There are other similarities," I continued. "You know how you can buy renewable, convertible term insurance? Well, disability policies come with similar guarantees. When you buy disability insurance, your best bet is a guaranteed renewable, non-cancellable policy. Write that down, Karin. This means that the policy can't be cancelled, that the company must renew it without a medical exam, and that the premium price can't go up for the length of the contract. That's the safest way to go."

"Let me guess, Charles," said Peter. "That's the most expensive kind of disability insurance."

"Correct," I replied. "There's no such thing as a free lunch. You could also go with guaranteed renewable insurance, which means that the premium could rise over the course of the contract, but it couldn't go up more for you than it would for everybody in the same class of insurance. And then there's commercial disability insurance. Here the company can change the price or decide it doesn't want to renew the policy. It's the cheapest, but as I've been saying —"

"You get what you pay for," they all chimed in.

"You guys learn fast," I said, chuckling.

"So," said Karin, "say I gross about $4,000 a month, give or take. How much is a guaranteed renewable, non-cancellable, et cetera, et cetera regular-occupation disability policy going to cost me?"

"Well, disability insurance ain't cheap," I said. "It's more expensive than several forms of life insurance. And that's partly because, as we've discussed, you're more likely to be disabled than you are to die prematurely. Karin, we can run an actual quotation on my laptop if you'd like, but I can tell you off the top of my head that a disability policy that pays out $2,600 a month, tax-free, will cost you approximately ninety dollars a month to age sixty-five, depending on the elimination period and your lifestyle and medical history."

"Why $2,600?" asked Daniel.

"Two-thirds of $4,000," answered Karin.

"That's expensive," said Lindsay.

"Yeah, but imagine what it would be like *not* to have it," said Karin.

"Exactly," I pointed out. "Although it's not small change, consider the alternatives. As we said, if you earn $4,000 a month, you'll have earned $3.2 million by the age of sixty-five. *That's* what the disability plan covers. We also talked about the fact that if you're disabled more than ninety days, it's likely that you'll be disabled for three years. Well, a disability benefit of $2,600 a month works out to just over $93,000 over the course of three years. And Karin, I have one suggestion for financing the cost of your insurance, at least in part."

"Suggest away," she said.

"Well, you mentioned you have mortgage insurance," I said. "But I can't see why you need it."

"What's mortgage insurance?" asked Daniel.

"It pays off your mortgage if you die," said Karin.

"Won't Daniel and I need mortgage insurance, then?" asked Lindsay. "Wait!" she answered herself. "We don't! We already covered the mortgage in our term insurance plans. Right?"

"Right," I said. "And that's good planning, because it's generally cheaper to add your mortgage costs to your term insurance policy than it is to take out an entirely separate policy just for your house."

"But why would you need to worry about mortgage insurance, Karin?" said Lindsay. "I mean, if you die, then the condo would be sold anyway, so the bank would get its money back from the proceeds of the sale."

"You know, I never really thought it through," said Karin. "It was just something my realtor and mortgage broker told me about, and I thought it sounded like a good deal at the time."

"Mortgage insurance only really makes sense, as Lindsay said, if you have dependants who will want to live in the house after your death, and who can't afford to pay off the mortgage themselves," I pointed out. "You might be better off putting the premiums you're paying for mortgage insurance towards a disability policy. It won't be nearly enough to cover the premiums, but it's a start."

"Are the premiums tax-deductible at least?" asked Karin.

"No," I replied.

"Why not?" asked my elder niece.

"Because the disability benefits are tax-free. It wouldn't be fair, in the eyes of the government, to let you deduct your premiums *and* not pay tax on your benefits."

"Okay, that makes sense," she said.

"How difficult is it to qualify for disability insurance?" Catherine wanted to know.

"Well, it's definitely not as easy as applying for life insurance," I said. "In fact, applying for private disability insurance is much more difficult. You won't necessarily be eligible for the policy you want, or for any insurance at all. The Canadian Life and Health Insurance Association has a booklet on disability insurance, and it breaks down the numbers. Up to 10 percent of applicants are rejected outright when they apply for insurance. Up to another 20 percent qualify, but they have some policy exclusions or their premiums are higher than average. And another 15 percent might qualify for policies with smaller benefits, longer elimination periods, or shorter benefit periods.

"As we've discussed, some people in risky professions are automatically disqualified. As well, if you had a pre-existing medical condition when you applied, you'd likely be turned down if that condition could potentially lead to a disability. Or you might be issued a policy that wouldn't pay benefits if you developed a disability because of that pre-existing condition. For the self-employed, it can be even harder, Karin. You have to prove that you work full time, and that you've established yourself in your industry. Often, you'll have to have been self-employed for at least three years — or more — before a company will issue you a policy."

"Why?" asked Catherine.

"Well, the insurance company wants a sense of your track record. They want to see that you've got a viable way of making an income before they'll insure your future earnings," I replied. "If you make a go of it as a freelance writer, for example, and never make a dime, you'll have a hard time proving that you qualify for disability benefits. On the other hand, if you have three or more years of tax returns and contracts that show a healthy self-employment income, you've got a better chance of qualifying."

"So someone just starting out as a freelancer or starting their own business wouldn't be able to get private disability insurance?" asked Peter.

"Probably not," I said. "It can be tough to buy without a proven record of income."

"So, Uncle Charles, where do you get this disability stuff, assuming you *can* get it?" asked Karin.

"The same place you get life insurance," I answered, "through a broker or an agent. You can check with your friends or colleagues to see if they have someone they'd recommend. And, Karin, if you belong to any professional associations, check with them. They might have a group association plan at slightly lower rates, as well as a better understanding of your profession and the risks specific to it. And check with your alumni association. It will often have group plans. Sometimes, though, alumni-association and similar plans have limits — they may cover only 50 percent of your income, for example, or come with fewer bells and whistles."

"I do belong to a couple of organizations," said Karin. "I'll check with them to see if they've got any deals."

"And when it comes to choosing a broker, the same rules apply for disability insurance as they do for life insurance:

you're going to have to trust this person with a lot of personal information, so make sure that you feel comfortable with him or her. Ask for references and check credentials."

"Charles," said my brother, "what about inflation? Three thousand dollars a month sounds pretty good right now, but it's not going to be worth much in ten or twenty years. Do these plans take inflation into account?"

"They can," I said. "You can purchase an inflation, or cost-of-living, rider with your policy. It's called a COLA for short, and it's designed to protect the value of your benefit from eroding because of inflation. I recommend it highly. At an inflation rate of 4 percent, three thousand dollars today will be worth about $2,000 in ten years. That's not a lot. Of course, the inflation rider will add to the cost of your insurance. In this case, however, I think the cost is worth it."

"Are there other riders?" asked Lindsay.

"Yup, lots," I answered. "Some of them, like the cost-of-living one, are potentially very valuable to you."

"Which ones would you recommend looking at, Uncle Charles?" asked Karin.

"Well, a waiver-of-premium rider means that you don't have to pay premiums while you're disabled. But it increases your costs over the long term. There's also a premium-refund rider, which means that if you don't make any claims over the course of your contract, the insurance company will refund all or part of your premiums after, say, ten or twenty years, depending on the policy."

"That sounds like a great deal," said Catherine.

"It's not bad," I said. "What it comes down to is weighing the cost of higher premiums against the chance that you will get back the cash you've put out over the years. For those of you who can't stomach the thought of paying for something you might never use, return of premium is a good rider."

"Of course, it's useless if you make a claim," said Karin.

"Correct," I said. "Ultimately, it's an individual decision. Return of premium is a very popular rider, however. It's kind of like the best of both worlds."

"Can you increase the amount of coverage you can get?" asked Peter. "I mean, Karin's been self-employed for only a couple of years, so the sky's the limit in terms of growth."

"Thanks for that vote of confidence, Dad," said Karin.

"You've got another good point," I said. "One very important rider ensures that you can buy more coverage if your income goes up. Let's say, Karin, that you buy a disability policy now. But in five years, your income has increased substantially. You'd want to make sure that you could buy additional coverage that matched your new higher earnings. That's called a future earnings option. Speaking of which, do you see your business expanding to include more people? A partner or some associates? An assistant or two?"

"Maybe one day," replied my niece. "I could certainly *use* an assistant. Why?"

"Well, you can also get disability insurance that covers your overhead expenses," I said. "Right now, it's just you working out of your condo, so I imagine that your overhead expenses aren't very high. But if you're paying salaries to employees, leasing equipment, or renting and maintaining an office, you have to think about whether your business would suffer major financial losses if you became disabled and couldn't run it on a day-to-day basis. It's something to think about as your business grows."

"Gee, I wonder if Lisa knows about this," said Catherine to Peter. Lisa, my eldest niece, was a businesswoman in her own right.

"We can ask her next week when she comes up," said Peter. "I'm sure she'll want to participate in the Stonehouse family insurance seminars as well."

"Uncle Charles, what about the government disability plans you were talking about?" asked Lindsay. "How do they fit it with private disability insurance? And how do you know if you qualify for them?"

"Well, the government generally has two kinds of disability plans for workers: short and long term," I said. "Short-term disability might mean that you need a month or two off to recover from an appendectomy or a broken arm that prevented you from doing your job. If you pay employment insurance premiums, then you qualify for short-term disability insurance through Human Resources Development Canada," I said.

"What if you have EI *and* private disability insurance?" asked Daniel.

"If you do have both, the private benefits will kick in after your elimination period is up — thirty, sixty, ninety or more days. And the government and your insurer will co-ordinate your benefits so that you still receive only two-thirds to three-quarters of your salary. And of course, your own plan will pay you for the duration of your contract or until you're able to go back to work, whichever comes first."

"And what are long-term government benefits like?" asked Catherine.

"Well," I answered, "they cover long-term disabilities. If your condition lasts more than a few weeks, you'll use up your short-term EI benefits. If you'd paid into the Canada or Quebec pension plans for the required number of years and you had a severe, prolonged disability, you'd be eligible for long-term disability benefits. CPP or QPP will pay up to age sixty-five, and will also pay extra benefits if you have dependent children. The benefit amount changes each year, but I believe the average amount is approximately $650, and the maximum amount you can receive goes up to about $900 or so."

"That's not much," commented Karin.

"No, it's not," I agreed. "It would be difficult to live on. If you have a private disability plan, however, you could supplement the government benefit. And again, if you have private disability insurance on top of your government benefits, the two sets of benefits will be co-ordinated. By the way, HRDC has a great web site that tells you all about its programs; I'll e-mail it to you."

"Well," said my sister-in-law, "I have a question. What about disability insurance for people like me? I didn't work outside the home when you children were growing up" — Catherine looked pointedly at her offspring — "but what would have happened if I'd become ill? We would have had to hire a cook, a nanny, a chauffeur, and a housekeeper to replace me."

"Not to mention a fashion consultant, tutor, peacekeeper, and moral authority," said Karin, smiling at her mother. "It would have cost a fortune."

"Well, Catherine, you've identified the problem with disability insurance, both government *and* private," I said. "It's designed to replace only earned, or employment, income, not necessarily the value of a person's work! So you can't buy it for someone, like a homemaker, who doesn't earn an income."

"Is there any option for people like us?" asked Catherine.

"Unfortunately, not really," I said. "The product that comes closest is relatively new. It's called critical illness insurance, and it's exactly what it sounds like. If you get diagnosed with a critical illness like cancer, heart disease, or multiple sclerosis, the insurance company pays you a lump sum, tax-free, to use as you see fit. In your case, you might have hired a nanny with the money. You could use it to keep paying down your mortgage, to pay for expensive therapies not covered under government plans, or even to go on vacation, if that's what you feel you need. In that sense, critical illness is more flexible than disability benefits."

"That's interesting," said Peter. "It feels a little bit like a gamble with the devil."

"I suppose you could look at it that way," I said. "But critical illness insurance is one way of making sure that you have some money to live off in the event of a tragedy. You can buy it in addition to life insurance — or in addition to disability insurance, for that matter. There's actually a neat story behind the product. Do you remember the doctor who performed the first human heart transplant?"

"Wasn't that in South Africa?" asked Peter. "In the late 1960s?"

"You're right," I said. "It was in 1967, and the doctor's name was Christiaan Barnard. He died just last year, I believe. Well, Christiaan's brother, Marius Barnard, was also a doctor, and he assisted his brother in the operation."

"Two geniuses in the family," remarked Peter slyly. "Their parents must have been very proud."

"What are you implying, Dad?" asked Lindsay.

"Anyway," I said, jumping in before things got out of hand. "Marius realized that as medicine advanced, people who would normally have died from critical diseases like heart disease and cancer were surviving longer and longer. Take heart attacks, for example. Since 1968, the immediate death rate from heart attacks has decreased by 51 percent. At the same time, the incidence of heart disease and the number of heart attacks have increased dramatically. The net result is that we're left with a lot more people recovering from heart attacks than in the past. These survivors often face financial hardship because they can't work, and they need care and treatment while they recover. The advances of medicine have created a modern medical dilemma: people are now living longer with critical illnesses, but they can't afford to do it."

"Imagine," said Karin, "you wake up from your operation, and the doctor says, 'The good news is that you'll live for another twenty years. The bad news is that you'll live the next twenty years in poverty because you won't be able to work.'"

"Exactly," I said. "Not a pretty thought. So Marius Barnard worked with the insurance industry to develop the concept of critical illness insurance. It's designed to get you through treatment and recovery until you can go back to work — if you have a job — or resume your day-to-day activities. And for people who don't qualify for disability benefits because they don't work, it's a viable alternative."

"So you get a disease, and you get the money?" said Lindsay.

"Not quite," I answered. "Not every disease is covered. Usually, the eligible diseases include cancer, heart attack, stroke, and multiple sclerosis. Those are the big four. And then insurance companies usually cover coronary artery bypass, paralysis, blindness or deafness, and . . . what are the other ones? Uh, kidney failure, Alzheimer's disease, and . . . and . . . oh, yes, Parkinson's disease. Different insurance companies include different illnesses."

"What about HIV or AIDS?" asked Catherine.

"If you contract HIV on the job, say through being stuck with a contaminated needle, it's usually covered," I replied. "But if you contract it off the job, as a sexually transmitted disease or through shared needles, for example, generally it's not covered. Again, what's covered depends on the insurance company itself."

"So life insurance covers your dependants in case you die," said Lindsay. "And critical illness covers you in case you live."

"Pretty much," I said. "In fact, some people who would never consider buying life insurance will buy critical illness coverage, even though it's more expensive. They're worried not about premature death, but about living too long, so to speak. Some people don't want or need to create an estate for their dependants; some people don't have any dependants. But if they get sick, they want a product that will help them while they're still alive and a burden, so to speak, to their families."

"How much does critical illness insurance cost?" asked Peter.

"Again, it varies according to the person applying for the insurance, the company, and the type of policy. Someone younger and in good health, obviously, will pay less than an older person. Non-smokers will pay less than smokers, and the insurance company will take into account your family history and your lifestyle. Then it depends on the terms of the policy: you can usually buy critical illness coverage for either a ten-year term or to age seventy-five. As well, you can choose a return-of-premium policy, which will refund all or part of the premiums if you don't make a claim."

"That makes it pretty risk-free, doesn't it?" asked Daniel.

"More or less," I replied. "Your capital is guaranteed. But there are some opportunity costs, too. You've preserved your capital, but your cost is the potential gains on your money had you invested it instead of paying premiums. Very little is entirely risk-free. But to get back to the question of costs, I recently sold a CI policy to a thirty-five-year-old woman in good health. She paid twenty-six dollars a month for $100,000 in coverage. That was for a ten-year return-of-premium policy."

"Can she renew the policy in another ten years?" asked Lindsay.

"Absolutely. You can buy CI as a guaranteed renewable policy, just like you can with term insurance. Of course, it'll be more expensive when and if she renews."

"Can you get critical illness insurance on top of life or disability insurance?" asked Daniel.

"Yes," I said, "you can. In fact, some life insurance companies market critical illness coverage as a rider. If you want both kinds of insurance, this might be a smart bet because if you have both policies rolled into one, you'll pay less money in policy fees. Still, it makes sense to shop around, so don't take the rider without comparing costs first."

"Who buys CI?" asked Karin. "I mean, how can you predict that you'll get cancer or develop a heart condition?"

"You can't, any more than you can predict that you'll die prematurely or become disabled," I answered. "People buy CI in order to make sure that they can maintain their lifestyle in the event they suffer a debilitating illness. And some people, like you said, Peter, buy it as a sort of gamble: 'Since I could get a disease, I might as well get a lump-sum payout if I *am* diagnosed.' A lot of the costs related to treating illness and rehabilitation aren't covered, or aren't covered fully, by our health-care system. And of course, if you can't work while you recover, you'll most likely run into financial problems. You can look at your family history and the stats on various illnesses, and decide if CI is something that feels right for you."

"What *are* the stats?" asked Lindsay.

"Well, you have to be careful about statistics," I replied. "Let's take cancer, for example. When my agents were selling critical illness insurance, we came across a brochure that said that one in three people will develop cancer during their lives. That seems very alarming, but the statistic is misleading in the sense that cancer tends to occur in people over the age of sixty. Forty-five percent of new cases and roughly 60 percent of cancer deaths occur in Canadians over the age of seventy, and another quarter or so of new cases and deaths occur in those in the sixty to sixty-nine group."

"Charles," said Catherine, "how do you keep all these numbers in your head?"

"I guess I have a bit of a photographic memory," I said. "Or literally a head for numbers. The point I'm trying to make is that you should do your own research on critical illness. Look at your family history of disease and get online. The Canadian Cancer Society, the Heart and Stroke Foundation, and the MS Society all have web sites. Or you can talk to your doctor, or another health-care professional, about the risks for certain diseases. And take a look at your own financial picture to decide how you'd cope with a severe illness.

"The other thing to consider if you have life insurance but don't have critical illness coverage is getting an advance on your death benefit. That's what's known as living benefits. It's depressing, but if you're diagnosed with a terminal illness, most insurance companies will grant you a loan against your death benefits. You can use the money from the death benefit to ease the financial hardships of your illness. I pray that none of you is ever in a position where you have to think about living benefits, but if the occasion arises, you should check with your insurance provider."

"Charles," said Peter, "what about us older folks? We might not have critical illnesses, but what about the results of simple ageing? What if I need help with everyday activities like cooking or cleaning or . . . getting dressed?"

There was an uncomfortable silence on the deck. The kids, I was pretty sure, didn't want to think about their parents becoming old and infirm, and none of us "geezers" relished the thought of the day when we'd have to give up some independence or lose some of our faculties. Still, it remained a distinct possibility. Here, the demographics are telling: more than one in ten Canadians is sixty-five or older. While most seniors live at home, many move to institutions as their mental and physical conditions deteriorate — in 1996, according to Statistics Canada, nearly 40 percent of women over eighty-five and one-quarter of their male counterparts lived in institutions.

"Well," I replied, "as the population ages, that's an increasingly important concern. That's where another product comes into play: long-term care. Unlike life insurance, where you're protecting your dependants in the event that you die too soon, the concern with long-term care is living for a long time without being able to perform the functions of everyday life. Long-term care insurance, as the name implies, is designed to help cover the expenses of health care over an extended period, at home or in an institution like an old-age home. And while long-term care insurance isn't cheap, the premiums can seem like small change when compared with the costs of a nursing home.

"You're all too young to be worried about long-term care right now," I told my nieces and nephew-in-law, who'd become considerably more sombre as they contemplated an old and frail future. "But keep it in mind for the future, if you don't think your savings alone will be enough to pay for the long-term care you may need. As for us geezers," I said, meaning myself, Peter, and Catherine, "it's something we've got to think long and hard about. But we can talk about that later."

"You're right, Uncle Charles," said Karin. "I've learned a ton about life insurance for the living today — disability benefits, critical illness, living benefits, long-term care — but after all, I *am* on vacation. Let's get on with the business of living! Who wants to go for a swim?"

RECIPES FOR SUCCESS

1 Your most valuable asset probably isn't
   that Maserati — it's your ability to earn a
   living! A thirty-five-year-old who makes
   $3,000 a month today will earn
   approximately $2.4 million by the age of sixty-five,
   assuming her earnings increase by 5 percent a year.
   If she earns $4,000 a month, her lifetime earnings
   will be more like $3.2 million. Disability insurance
   helps to protect that earnings potential.

2 Your eligibility for disability insurance — and the
   cost of your premiums — will depend on a variety
   of factors, including your health, how much you earn,
   your occupation, and the type of coverage you buy.

3 While disability benefits are tax-free, you can
   generally receive up to two-thirds of your current
   income in benefits.

4 The concept of critical illness insurance was
   invented by Dr. Marius Barnard, who assisted his
   brother, Dr. Christiaan Barnard, with the first heart
   transplant. Marius was aware of the financial impact
   a critical illness could have on a patient: this type
   of coverage pays out a lump-sum benefit if you are
   diagnosed with one of several serious illnesses, like
   heart disease, cancer, or multiple sclerosis.

5 If you're diagnosed with a terminal disease, you
   might be able to receive living benefits: an advance
   on your life insurance benefits.

7

BUSINESS BASICS:

LIFE INSURANCE FOR THE TYCOON IN ALL OF US

"AHA! It's my niece the computer whiz! When did you arrive?"

Lisa looked up from her laptop as I entered the kitchen, shopping bags in hand. I had made a run to pick up a few things from the grocery store. We were low on flour, and I wanted to try out a new recipe in the bread-maker: coffee cake.

"Hi, Uncle Charles," said my eldest niece, getting up from the table to give me a hug. "I just got here. But where are my parents?"

"They went into town for some kind of cottage-owners community meeting," I said. "Something your father was interested in: bringing high-speed Internet access to cottage country! They should be back in about an hour."

"Neat," said Lisa. "If we had high-speed access, maybe I could come up here for longer visits and do some work. You know, a kind of virtual office." She looked at her humming laptop. "Like I need to do more work. I promised myself I wasn't going to do any work this weekend, but no one was here, and there were just a few things I had to —" Her cellphone rang.

"Oh, man!" Lisa looked at the call display on the tiny phone as I chuckled. "I really have to get this one — it's the office, and I told Denise to call me if there were any problems," she said, heading for the patio. "Excuse me for one second."

I watched her through the window with a grin as she talked and gestured. Lindsay and Daniel had gone back to Ottawa two weeks earlier in preparation for the baby, and Karin's visit had been too brief. During the "down time" between nieces and nephews, I had finished *War and Peace* (not a small accomplishment), played more chess, and experimented with new bread recipes. Peter, Catherine, and I had done our fair share of hiking, canoeing, and relaxing. But the cottage had begun to feel a bit empty, so I was more than happy to see my first-born niece, who was also here for just a few days.

Lisa has always been a go-getter. Maybe it's got to do with being the eldest child. She excelled in school, especially in math and science — even skipped a grade early on. She went to university on a full scholarship and then, like her father, got her M.B.A. while working full time, in her case at a software company. Along the way, she met and married Michel, a French-Canadian aerospace scientist. They had two kids, Oscar and Rachel, both of whom seem to take after their intellectual parents. And they're bilingual to boot.

Unfortunately, Lisa and Michel separated about a year ago. Now they're going ahead with the divorce. Both were working crazy hours — he for Bombardier and she with a couple of partners in a startup company, building software that links remote computer systems. I guess that by the time they realized they had grown apart, it was too late. They've been pretty amicable about things, but from what I hear via Peter and Catherine, Lisa had a rough time for a while. Now, however, the worst seems to be over. And the kids, by all accounts, are adjusting well.

Out of this cloud of upheaval, however, has come a silver

lining: all those hours Lisa put into her company for the past few years are paying off. They've got several deals with established technology and computer firms. What's more, they even have a product, which is more than I can say for some of the dot-com companies of recent years. I could just see it: my niece, the Canadian Bill Gates!

Lisa returned to the kitchen.

"I am turning this cellphone *off* for the weekend," she said, doing just that. "And the same goes for the computer. I'm here to relax!"

"How goes it in the corporate jungle?" I asked.

"Great, Uncle Charles," she replied as she saved files and shut down the computer. "It's been a hectic few months. We got a call from a very large company in the spring, and there's been talk of an alliance of some kind. I wish I could say more, but we've signed a non-disclosure agreement."

"You mean a buyout? A merger?"

"I don't know just yet," she said mysteriously. "Or at least I can't really talk about it in too much detail. It's still pretty early, but I wouldn't say either of those options is out of the question. Needless to say, we're all kind of excited. But we're trying to keep our heads about us, too."

"Great! Where are the kids?"

"They're with Michel this weekend. We're working out a pretty liveable custody arrangement. They'll be up here with me at the end of summer. You know, for the annual Labour Day weekend party."

"So that's all going relatively smoothly?" I asked, unloading my shopping bags onto the kitchen counter.

"As smoothly as ending a marriage goes, I guess," my niece replied. "Actually, I meant to talk to you about a couple of the decisions we've made. I thought you'd be interested. We've done a neat thing with our life insurance policies. . . . But what are you making?" she asked, looking at the bread-maker. "And how does that thing work?"

I began to show Lisa the ins and outs of my retirement gift. As I tossed in some milk, an egg yolk, butter, flour, and the rest of the ingredients, my niece — ever the engineer — examined the inner workings of the machine.

"That's fascinating," she said. "Kinda takes the romance out of making bread, though, doesn't it?"

"I suppose you could think of it that way. For me, it takes the *work* out of making bread," I replied, closing the top of the bread-maker and pressing the Dough setting. The machine whirred noisily into action as it began to knead together the ingredients. "And that's good enough for me. But I'm curious to know about your life insurance decisions."

"Well, my attorney came up with what I think is a really smart strategy," said Lisa. "Michel and I always had life insurance on each other, thanks to your advice! But now, with the divorce, things could get pretty awkward. Since I have custody, he's paying me child support. I need that money, and if he dies prematurely, I'll need the death benefit. And the same would apply for him if I died prematurely and he had to take the kids. So, obviously, we need to keep the policies on each other's lives as a condition of the divorce. But what if he cancels the policy on his life or doesn't make the payments and lets it lapse? I'd be in a lot of trouble without any insurance."

"So what have you done?" I asked.

"Well, I've taken out a twenty-year term policy on him, and he's taken one out on me. I own the policy on him, I pay the premiums, and I'm the irrevocable beneficiary. He's done the same thing. So now we're both financially protected in case one of us dies prematurely, and we're both in control of that protection. Since I pay for the policy, I'll never have to hound him to make the premium payments, and I don't have to worry about his cancelling the policy, because it belongs to me. And I know the kids will be looked after either way."

"That *is* clever," I said. "You've got a smart family lawyer."

"I do," she said. "And I suppose that if this merger or buyout ball really gets rolling, I'll need an equally smart business attorney, someone in mergers and acquisitions."

"Well," I said, "get someone who's as knowledgeable about insurance as your divorce lawyer. A lot of insurance issues come up in business, whether you're merging or not."

"What kind of insurance issues? We've got a group health plan in place for everyone at the office, and we've got some disability coverage through the same insurance company, which covers the partners and the business," said Lisa. "What else do we need?"

"You're talking primarily about health and disability insurance for you and your employees and partners. But I'm talking about life insurance — for the health of your company, so to speak. There's a difference."

"What do you mean?" asked Lisa.

"Well, how many partners do you have?" I asked, setting out the ingredients for the coffee cake's topping.

"There are three of us," said Lisa, popping a pecan into her mouth. "I deal with sales and marketing, Denise handles the technological end, and Lorne deals with all the finances."

"What would happen if one of you became seriously disabled or died? Could you continue the day-to-day operations of the company if one of you left suddenly?" I mixed together half a cup of sugar with some cinnamon and the pecans.

"Oh!" Lisa looked startled. "I wonder if we could. It would be hard, in any case. The three of us get along really well, and we all do such different things. I don't know if we could continue to run seamlessly. We'd probably need to hire someone else, but that would take time."

"And money," I said. "You'd have to pay top dollar, I imagine, to find someone with the necessary skills."

"Yeah," she said. "I imagine we would. And we don't have a lot of liquid cash just lying around. I mean, we're not doing badly at all, but all our money is tied up in product and inventory, not to mention loans. We're worth a fair amount on paper, but we're a bit cash-poor."

"That's the classic situation for new businesses," I said. "Your company's in its infancy, which means that you've got low cash levels, not a lot of financial leverage with banks or other lenders, high risk levels — and to balance that, a lot of energy and potential! You need insurance to help manage your risks and protect your business so it can achieve its potential. And one important part of managing risk is making sure that you protect your key players. So one of the first uses of insurance for your business would be to replace one of your partners in the event of death or disability. In the industry, we talk about 'key man' insurance, although in your case 'key woman' would certainly be applicable."

"How does it work?" asked Lisa.

"It's very simple, actually," I answered. "You and your partners would sit down, perhaps with your accountant or a human-resources specialist if you felt it was necessary, and come up with the amount of money you think you'd need to hire someone with the right skill set and experience to replace any one of you. Then you take out life insurance policies, one for each of you, for that amount. In case of premature death, you have the cash on hand to hire someone else. It still won't be an easy thing, but key man . . . sorry, person insurance makes it easier."

"And what if one of us became disabled?" asked Lisa.

"Well, there is 'key person' disability insurance, but as with any other kind of disability insurance, there are limits on how much you can receive in benefits; it's usually a percentage of the insured's salary. If your partners are insured, you might not qualify for much more in the way of disability coverage. So the short answer is that you'll have a tougher time coming up with the money to replace a key player who's disabled. If you're really worried, you could take out critical illness insurance on each partner. That way, if any of you contracted or developed a serious illness covered by the policy, the business would receive a lump sum of cash. On the other hand, you don't want to burden yourselves with too much in the way of premium expenses."

"You know," said Lisa, "I guess we've just been so swamped with work that it never occurred to any of us to think about what would happen if all three of us weren't doing it together. I guess we should look into 'key man,' or 'key woman,' coverage."

I sat down at the kitchen table. "The three of you get along quite well, don't you?"

"Oh, it's great." Lisa smiled as she leaned back in her chair. "I was a little worried that going into business together would ruin the friendships, but it's made them stronger. Getting the company going has been so intense, and we put in so many hours. If we didn't all like each other as much as we do, it could have been really frustrating. Plus" — she shook her head a little ruefully — "they've been really supportive during my separation."

"Well, that's the second thing you should think about," I said. "The three of you have done so well, at least in part, because you like each other so much and work well together. But in the event that one of you dies, you risk losing that dynamic."

"Well, obviously," said Lisa. "I mean, one of us would be gone."

"More than that," I countered. "You could find yourself with a new business partner, someone you never hired or wanted to work with."

"What do you mean?" asked my niece, alarmed.

"Well, take Lorne. Is he involved with anyone?"

"Yeah. He's been married for about five years."

"In the very unfortunate event that Lorne got hit by a bus tomorrow, have you thought about what would happen to his shares in the company?"

"Well, he owns a third of it, technically," said Lisa. "Is that why you asked if he was involved? Would his wife get his shares?"

"Yes, unless he — or you, as the company — had made other arrangements," I answered. "Without the proper agreements and funding in place, you could find yourself with a new partner in business: the surviving spouse."

"That's crazy!" said Lisa. "I mean, I really like Lorne's wife, but I wouldn't want to be in business with her. And I highly doubt that she'd be interested in taking over his job, let alone be qualified to do it!"

"My point exactly," I replied. "But say she did become your new partner. You have two options: you can either work with her or buy her out — *if* she agrees to be bought out."

"I guess we'd have to buy her out," said Lisa.

"But your money's all tied up," I pointed out. "You said that yourself. Plus, you've got to factor in the potential for enormous growth. If your merger or buyout goes through, you could be worth several millions of dollars overnight, at least on paper. You'd have to consider if you could afford to buy her out."

"I'm beginning to see your point," said Lisa. "The three of us need to take out life insurance on each other, right? That way, if one of us dies, the other two can buy back the surviving spouse's share of the business."

"You're right," I said.

"So how do we do it?" she asked. "I mean, how can we know at any given time what the business is worth? And how can we make sure that the spouse will agree to sell his or her shares? And for the right price?"

"Well, to quote Maria von Trapp, let's start at the very beginning," I said. "The first thing you'd do is sit down with your accountant and figure out the fair market value of the business. That would be what the business is worth today — what it would fetch on the open market at arm's length."

"What's arm's length?" asked my niece.

"I mean what the business would be worth to an outsider — someone without an emotional stake in the company. Got it?"

"I'm with you so far," said Lisa, smiling.

"Great. So you'd figure out the fair market value. Then the three of you would draft and sign what's called a buy-sell agreement, which would include a promissory note. In this agreement, you mutually stipulate that if any one of you dies, the surviving partners will buy the deceased's shares at fair market value. A promissory note is a signed, written promise, pure and simple, in which you agree to pay, on request or within a specified amount of time, a certain amount of money to a designated person."

"Fair enough," said Lisa.

"Now, you've promised to buy out these shares. But in the event that one of you dies, where will you get the money? The next step is to find a way to fund your buy-sell agreement."

"Oh!" said Lisa, a light going on in her eyes. "We get the money by taking out life insurance policies on each one of us for the fair market value of the business! Right?"

"Actually, since there are three of you, you'd each be insured for a third of the value of the business, plus a bit more, for reasons I can explain later. So if the company is valued at, say, $3 million, then you'd each have million-dollar-plus policies. The company is the beneficiary of the policies. If one of you dies, then the company is paid the death benefit, tax-free. It then uses the death benefit to buy back the shares from the deceased's estate."

"What if the surviving spouse doesn't want to sell his or her shares?" asked Lisa.

"It doesn't matter," I answered, "because of the promissory note. Since you and your partners have signed the note, it stands. The spouse has to accept the money and relinquish his or her shares in the business."

"And what about taxes?" asked Lisa.

"What about them?"

"Well, I know that death benefits are tax-free to the beneficiary. But in this case, the company is the beneficiary, right? So *we* wouldn't have to pay tax on the benefit. But when we use the money to buy out, say, Lorne's widow, doesn't she have to pay tax on it?"

"That's a good question," I replied. "But in fact, she wouldn't. What happens is that in the year of death of one of the business partners, your accountant would create a notional account called a capital dividend account, or CDA. That's a one-time-only account that's set up for precisely this situation. The death benefit would be paid into the CDA, and it would pay out the benefits to Lorne's wife in the form of tax-free dividends. So she would get her money tax-free in the end."

"I get it," said Lisa. "That's simple enough."

"It's a pretty good system," I said, "and in the end, it works quite well for a number of reasons. First of all, buy-sell agreements take a lot of the emotion out of what could potentially be some pretty overwrought situations. Without an agreement covering how much the business is worth and who will and won't be a party in running it, you'd be surprised at how things can get out of hand. I've seen situations where a widow or widower is convinced that the business is worth much more than the surviving partners believe it to be, and cases where the widow or widower decides that he or she wants to take an active hand in controlling how the company is run, much to the dismay of the surviving partners. In the absence of an agreement, the remaining partners can also often buy out the surviving spouse for too much money and then find that the business is hard up for cash. These cases can often end up in court: close friendships are severed, and good businesses can go down the drain."

"Yuck," said Lisa.

"Exactly," I replied. "It's much easier to take care of things beforehand — kind of like having a will. By the way, I assume that you and Michel have updated your wills since the separation, right?"

"Yes, Uncle Charles," said Lisa dutifully. "That's all taken care of."

"Sorry. I shouldn't pry. I just like to make sure of these things — it's habit. But back to the subject at hand. Another advantage of buy-sell agreements is that banks tend to look upon them favourably. They're always happy to know that their clients are covered, and they even look upon these arrangements as assets. So if your bank knows that you and your partners are covered in the event of premature death, it might just give you a little more leverage."

"Interesting," said Lisa. "That's good to know. Banks are a lot more suspicious these days of computer startups than they were before the stock-market bust. Any bit of extra pull can't hurt."

"My sentiments exactly," I replied. "There are a couple of disadvantages to buy-sell agreements, however, although the advantages tend to outweigh them. For example, there's the burden of premium costs. That's simple: the more people you're insuring and the more policies you have, the more expensive it's going to get. Younger companies, or even older ones, aren't necessarily in the best position to afford those expenses. As well, buy-sell agreements get more complicated as the number of stakeholders grows. Since there are only three of you, your agreement should be relatively straightforward. But imagine, say, a law firm with fifty partners. Its buy-sell agreements would be way tougher to implement."

"There are some advantages to being a small company," said Lisa. "Hey, are those premium costs tax-deductible?"

"Unfortunately, no. Because the death benefit is tax-free, you can't deduct the premiums from your otherwise taxable income. The only time you can deduct some of the premiums is for collateral insurance."

"And that would be what?" asked Lisa.

"Well, say you want a million-dollar bank loan to finance building a new warehouse for the company," I suggested. "The bank is willing to give you the money, but only if you take out a million-dollar insurance policy that guarantees the loan in the event of the death of one of the partners. Since you're required to take out insurance as a condition of borrowing money for business reasons, you can deduct part of the premium costs as a business expense — as long as the company, that is, not you, is the owner and the beneficiary of the policy."

"So if I'm required to buy insurance as a condition of borrowing money for the business, I can deduct the premiums," said Lisa.

"Exactly. You can't deduct the entire amount, however — just what's known as the net cost of pure insurance. The NCPI, as it's called, is determined by the Canada Customs and Revenue Agency, formerly known as good old Revenue Canada. The premiums for insurance policies are made up of the NCPI, plus the company's overheads and issue costs. The NCPI is equivalent to approximately one year of term insurance costs."

"How would I find out how much we could deduct, then?" asked Lisa.

"You could find out from the CCRA," I said. "But your insurance company should be able to tell you. The net cost of pure insurance, by the way, also figures into the amount of life insurance you need to buy to cover the terms of your buy-sell agreement. Remember that I said you'd have to buy a bit more coverage than your third of the business's value?"

"Uh-huh."

"Well, that's because the amount in the capital dividend account won't necessarily equal the full amount of the death benefit. In fact, tax rules dictate that it'll contain the death benefit, *less* the ACB, or adjusted cost base, of the policy. That's the difference between the premiums you've paid and the NCPI. For example, if you've paid $100,000 in premiums, but the NCPI is actually $85,000, then $15,000 will be taxed. So if you don't slightly overfund your insurance policy, you might find that you have a shortfall if and when it comes time to buy out a surviving spouse. It's a niggling detail, but you should know about it — at least, your accountant should."

"Wow," said Lisa. "We've got ACBs, CDAs, NCPIs — good thing I work in acronyms all day long anyway. You've been talking about term insurance. Does that mean you think that's the type of policy we should get?"

"Definitely — at least for now," I replied. "The whole point of using life insurance to fund 'key person' or buy-sell agreements is that it's a cost-effective way to do it. Because you're a young business, you don't have to have the money on hand to buy out a partner's spouse or estate, so insurance is a practical solution. And at the outset, term insurance tends to be the least expensive kind of insurance you can buy. In the future, however, you might have enough in the way of liquid assets that you won't need the term insurance to fund the policy."

"That would be nice," said Lisa.

"Well, with the way things are going for you guys, it's certainly within the realm of possibility in the very near future. Actually, there are a lot of possibilities for the future. In five or ten years — even less! — if you play your cards right, you and your partners might find yourselves with a large, prosperous company and lots of cash to play with. Or, hey, Microsoft might call tomorrow, and you could find yourselves instant millionaires."

"Or we could win the lottery," said Lisa.

"I think my examples are much more realistic," I said. "However you come by it, when you find yourselves with more cash to spare — and more tax to pay — you can start looking at using universal life insurance to protect your company, benefit partners, *and* maybe even defer some taxes. Are you familiar with universal life?"

"Well, I wasn't until Andrew phoned up and told me about his insurance session with you," said Lisa, laughing. "He was pretty excited about the concept   the idea that you could get nearly tax-free savings and retirement income."

"Well, I'm glad to hear the word gets around, I guess," I said, a little embarrassed. "I'm worried that I've become the insurance uncle. As long as you're saying good things . . ."

"Oh, don't worry! We are," said my niece, putting her hand on mine. "Andrew said that he and Rebecca found your advice really useful. And apparently Lindsay's turned into a life insurance convert. She can't figure out why no one taught her this stuff before! Karin, too. When I talked to her last week, she was applying for disability insurance. She said that you made it really easy to understand, and that no one had ever told her of the risks of disability. Now I guess it's my turn for one of Uncle Charles's insurance seminars. So tell me why I should use universal life."

"I'm not saying you should, just that it's an option for the future." I paused. "Now I feel silly — I've managed to corral you into a 'seminar' within the first hour of your arrival."

"As I recall, *I* was the one who brought up life insurance," said Lisa. "I told you about my arrangements with Michel. Don't worry! This is interesting — and kind of fun."

Her words put me at ease. "All right," I said, pretending to be gruff. "But only because you asked."

"Fair enough," said my niece. "Now where were we?"

"We were talking about how you could use universal life as your business grows," I said. "Specifically, I'm thinking about something called a split-dollar arrangement. In a nutshell, that's when you and your company split both the costs and the benefits of life insurance. You can use any kind of permanent insurance policy for a split-dollar arrangement, but universal life policies work especially well because they're already divided into two main components: the death benefit, or face value, and the cash value. This makes it particularly easy to figure out who's responsible for which costs and who receives which benefit."

"When would you use split-dollar?" asked Lisa.

"In theory, you can use a split plan for pretty much any type of situation," I said. "Parents, for example, might use split-dollar insurance to invest for themselves while providing their children with inexpensive, permanent life insurance. You can use it to fund buy-sell agreements, too. In terms of business, however, it's particularly useful as a way of funding key-man, or key-person, agreements. Depending on how you structure the plan, split-dollar can provide a company and its key players with either permanent life insurance at term prices or the opportunity to accumulate wealth, virtually tax-free — or in some cases, both."

"How does it work?" Lisa was intrigued.

"Well, the standard split-dollar arrangement is that an individual takes out a life insurance policy and splits the premium costs with his or her company. Then when the insured dies, the death benefit and any cash value in the policy are divided between the company and the insured's estate. That way, the company gets coverage for its key employee, and the employee gets life insurance."

"That sounds pretty simple," said Lisa. "But what about accumulating wealth and getting cheap permanent life insurance?"

"Well," I answered, "that's where universal life comes in. I guess Andrew explained to you that the premiums for universal life are flexible. You have to put in a minimum amount, and you can overfund the policy up to a certain maximum. Anything up to that maximum grows tax-deferred until it's withdrawn from the policy."

"Yeah," said Lisa. "That's what Andrew was so excited about."

"It can be very lucrative," I said, "and it can be especially lucrative for businesses. With universal life, a corporation can own the cash-value portion of the policy and the employee can own the life-insurance component. That's known as the conventional split-dollar arrangement. Here, the employee would pay the minimum amount required to cover the costs of the life insurance and the corporation would overfund the policy beyond the minimum."

"So the employee gets permanent life insurance at roughly the cost of term insurance," began Lisa.

"And the company gets to accumulate tax-deferred wealth while recovering the costs incurred for the policy," I finished. "If the employee dies, his or her beneficiary gets the death benefit and the corporation receives the cash sur-render value — tax-free, of course. It can then use the cash to replace its key employee, if necessary. And of course, if the policy has had a chance to mature, there might well be a lot of built-up value in that account."

"Smart!" Lisa was impressed.

"Isn't it? It's quite tidy, really. But there's yet another spin on split-dollar insurance. You can reverse the benefits: the corporation can be the death-benefit owner and the employee or shareholder can own the cash value. Here, the employee has access to the tax-deferred investment account, and the corporation gets its key-person insurance in the form of the death benefit — essentially, it's getting permanent insurance at term costs."

"So the company would pay the minimum amount and the employee could put in anything up to the maximum?" asked Lisa. I could practically see the wheels whirring in her brain.

"Exactly," I said. "So for an executive, a reverse split-dollar arrangement could be a very lucrative thing. Say you've maxed out your RRSPs and any other tax-deferral options open to you — like RESPs for the kids. Well, you've run out of ways to save for your retirement and defer taxes. If you've got the cash to invest in it, a universal life plan is a very good option. And it's made even better because your company is paying the minimum. I had clients who put up to $10,000 a year into plans like these. If they died, the company would get the death benefit, which it could use to hire someone else. And the insured's beneficiaries got the cash value — again, tax-free."

"But what if they lived?" asked Lisa.

"Good for them!" I replied. "It gets better. If the employee lives until retirement, well, then the company no longer needs the death benefit. So it will want to stop paying the premiums. But the retired employee might very well want the extra coverage. Well, for one measly dollar, the company can transfer its interest in the death-benefit portion of the policy to the employee upon his or her retirement. Now the employee has the option of owning not only the cash value, but also the face value, or death benefit, of the policy. And although he or she will have to start paying the premiums, remember that someone else — namely, the company — has been paying them all these years. It's a better retirement gift than a gold watch, really."

"Or a bread-maker?" asked Lisa coyly.

"Nope," I said. "I wouldn't trade my retirement gift for the world. But believe me, I wouldn't turn down extra insurance coverage if I needed it."

"So once our executive has retired, according to what Andrew said, he or she can use the built-up cash value in the UL policy as collateral for a bank loan, right?" said Lisa. "He or she can then live off the loan, pay a low interest rate, and avoid the higher tax hit that would come from cashing in the policy."

"You've got it!" I said. "No wonder you skipped a grade.

It's a good deal for both parties. For the employee — say, a CEO or another key shareholder, like the owner of a small business — a reverse split-dollar policy can be a great way to enhance retirement savings. At the same time, his or her company is covered in case of the key employee's death. And a hidden advantage is that these kinds of plans are excellent retainment strategies: a key employee might be less inclined to leave a firm when she's got generous benefits, like the opportunity to participate in a split-dollar insurance policy."

"Makes sense," said Lisa. "So how do you go about setting up one of these things? It might make a lot of sense for us — not necessarily now, but in a few years."

"It's very easy to set up," I said. "There are a few steps to the process. The first is that the employee must apply for, and receive, a universal life insurance policy. That employee names his or her beneficiary and pays the first month's premium. After the insurance is issued, *then* the employee and his or her company will sit down and create a split-dollar agreement. In that agreement, they'll set out their respective rights and obligations regarding the policy — essentially, who's responsible for which part of the payment and who receives what in the event of death. You know, fun stuff like that."

"Gotcha," said my niece. "So at that point, they'd decide whether it was a conventional split-dollar agreement or a reverse one?"

"Precisely," I said. "Once the agreement has been drafted and signed, the employee signs the necessary forms that assign, or transfer, the contract into joint ownership with the company. The insurance agent will help with all this. Then both parties designate their beneficiaries. At that point, if we're dealing with a corporation, the corporate board will usually have to approve the agreement. Once they've agreed, you're home free — well, almost. The final step is to specify power of attorney; since the insurance policy is now jointly owned property, both parties in the deal need to agree on what will happen to it if the insured becomes ill or incapacitated."

"Hello! Lisa!" Catherine and Peter walked into the kitchen.

The next few minutes were taken up with the latest parent-child reunion. Peter was excited about the community meeting and the possibility of "wiring" the Gatineaus. Once he spotted Lisa's brand-new laptop, however, the two computer engineers were lost in their own special world. Like father, like daughter. They disappeared into Peter's study as Catherine, beaming, grabbed her latest novel and prepared to head down to the dock to sunbathe and read.

"Coming, Charles?" she asked me.

The bread-maker began its familiar pinging, letting me know my dough was ready.

"In a minute," I told my sister-in-law. "I just need to put together this cake and then I'll meet you out there."

RECIPES FOR SUCCESS

1   If you're separating or divorcing,
    consider buying an insurance policy on
    your ex's life to protect child-support
    payments and the costs of raising the
    kids. Since you own the policy and pay
    the premiums, you're in control.

2   Like families, businesses have life insurance needs.
    Could your company function without one of its key
    players? If your business partner died prematurely,
    would the company have the funds to buy back his
    or her shares from the estate? If you answered no to
    either question, you might need to consider key-man
    insurance and buy-sell agreements.

3   Split-dollar arrangements use universal life insurance
    to protect a company against the loss of key employees,
    benefit employees, and maybe even defer some taxes.
    Here, a company and its employee split the costs and
    the benefits of universal life insurance.

8

RETIRING IN STYLE:

MAXIMIZING RETIREMENT WEALTH AND MINIMIZING TAXES WITH LIFE INSURANCE

"ADULTS ONLY: Absolutely no one under fifty allowed on these premises."

Peter, Catherine, and I joked about nailing such a sign on the cottage's front door, at least until Labour Day weekend. On that last official weekend of summer, and the cottage season, the entire Stonehouse clan — parents, kids, grandchildren, nieces, nephews, and pretty much anyone else — would descend upon the cottage for an annual barbecue and party.

Until then, however, only the over-fifty set would be around. We were now into the second week of August, and I couldn't believe how quickly the summer had passed. Lisa's retreat from the corporate world had been a brief but lovely long weekend. Her departure marked the end of "the onslaught of children," as Peter had jokingly put it.

"Just us geezers now," he had said, waving as Lisa's car pulled out of the driveway. "Now we can get out that sixteen-year-old Scotch."

My brother did a good job of bluffing, but I knew he was always sorry to see any of his offspring leave. When he and Lisa weren't talking technology, they were fishing off the end of the dock. Catherine had also spent a good few hours with her eldest daughter, hiking and catching up. Peter and Catherine had obviously taken Lisa's unhappiness over the breakup of her marriage to heart. At the same time, they were absolutely thrilled at her business successes. I also knew that the Labour Day weekend was one of their favourite times of the year: both of them lit up just at the thought of being surrounded by all the kids and grandchildren.

I was looking forward to the party myself, although I knew it would mark yet another transition for me. The summer up in the Gatineau Hills had been the perfect post-retirement strategy. When I returned to the city, however, I'd have to come up with ways to keep myself busy. But I had been thinking about my options during long walks through the woods and in evenings watching sunsets. I even had a couple of plans.

Those plans, however, would have to stay on hold for a little while because Peter, Catherine, and I were preparing for the next and final set of weekend guests. My baby sister, Joyce, and her husband, Rob, would be arriving shortly.

Joyce is fifty-five. She was a bit of a "miracle baby" for my parents, born when I was eight years old and Peter was eleven. I'm sure my mother had resigned herself to the thought that she'd have only two children — and no daughters. So she and my father were both surprised and elated at my sister's arrival: hence, the name Joyce. Peter and I were pretty happy, too. Joyce tells us that we were only very occasionally slightly overprotective. By the time she was old enough to get into serious trouble, however, both of us had left home: Peter to RMC and me to work.

Being the baby by a considerable margin also meant that Joyce grew up at a time when my parents had a bit more cash to spare. They could afford to send her to the University of Toronto, where she did a bachelor's degree in science and was then admitted to medical school, one of a handful of young women in her class. That's where she met Rob, who was doing a degree at the university's law school. They married after graduation. She's had a successful career as a general practitioner, and he's a partner at a downtown Toronto law firm, specializing in mergers and acquisitions. They have two boys, Spencer, who's twenty-eight, and Fraser, twenty-five. Spence has followed in his father's footsteps and is a second-year associate in a law firm; Fraser is a graphic artist and web page designer. One of his first big jobs was getting Rob's firm on-line.

I hadn't seen my sister and Rob since the previous Christmas, which I had spent at their house in North Toronto, so I was looking forward to their arrival. The weekend promised to be beautiful — and decadent. We had booked a tee time on Sunday, and would spend the rest of the weekend lounging, eating, and enjoying the outdoors and each other's company. I couldn't wait.

♦ ♦ ♦

"So, Charles," said Joyce, leaning forward in her deck chair, "Catherine tells me you've been baking bread and dispensing financial advice from on high all summer long. I hear the kids have got quite the lesson in life insurance."

"And we're all gaining weight," added Peter.

Joyce and Rob had arrived at about noon. Now we were enjoying some appetizers on the deck. Dinner would consist of marinated chicken breasts and grilled vegetables done on the barbecue. True to form, I'd made a batch of whole-wheat dinner rolls.

"Yes, Charles has moved on to educating the second generation," said Catherine. "You know, Charles, I still remember when you explained to me and Peter how life insurance worked. And now Lindsay and Daniel have had the same lesson."

"I wish you'd give it to our kids," said Rob. "They're pretty much in the dark when it comes to managing money.

Fraser's getting a bit better at the whole thing because he's running his own business. But Spence is too busy at work to even think about it right now."

"Next time I'm in Toronto, I'll set up a seminar or two," I joked. "Too bad they couldn't come up to the cottage this summer and sit in."

"Well, if the advice you've given the kids is half as good as the advice you've given me and Rob over the years, they're getting a very valuable service," declared Joyce. "Our universal life plan is going great guns. I'm actually thinking of retiring earlier than I had planned, and I think we'll have the money to do it."

"Great," I said. "But I'm not surprised. You two took a really aggressive approach to that investment. Actually, I told Andrew and Rebecca to give you a call to talk about universal life. Have they?"

"Not yet," said Joyce.

"I know they've talked to Lisa about it," said Catherine. "They're just exploring options right now. I didn't know that you and Rob had gone the UL route, Joyce."

"Oh, yes," she said. "Years ago. We sat down with Charles and figured out a financial plan, thought about our retirement goals —"

"Early!" interjected Rob.

"Exactly," continued his wife, "and how we could save for them. We also had a bit of money to play with from Rob's parents' estate, so it seemed like a good time to figure out the next steps. Charles told us about universal life."

"So," said Peter, "I don't want to pry, but just how lucrative has this policy been for you?"

"Well," said Joyce carefully, "we took out a universal life policy ten years ago, when I was forty-five. We've put $15,000 a year into the policy every year, and we'll keep contributing for another five years. At this point, the total cash value of the policy is around $250,000. The death benefit is somewhere around $900,000. At the rate we're going, by the time I'm sixty years old, the policy will have more than half a million dollars in cash value, and a death benefit of $1.2 million."

"Whoa!" said Peter. "Fifteen thousand dollars a year? And $1.2 million in death benefits? That's a lot of cash."

"It is," said Joyce. "It's our most aggressive investment, after our RRSPs. But Rob's done well over the years, and I don't make a bad living, so we were able to come up with the cash every month. And it's grown on its own. Trust me — I'm as astounded as you."

There was a slightly uncomfortable silence. Even among the most open of families, I've found, talking about money can be awkward.

"Joyce and Rob originally had quite a high death benefit," I said, steering the conversation back on track. "Spencer and Fraser were still relatively young when you took out the policy, so you guys needed a lot of insurance coverage."

"Right," said Rob. "I think the original death benefit was $500,000. But wasn't the policy designed to decrease the death benefit as we got older, Charles?"

"Well, yes and no," I said. "You went with a 'wealth maximizer' policy. Essentially, what it means is that the death benefit begins to decrease after the fifth year the policy's in force. Therefore, the costs of insurance decreased to the lowest amount allowable, with the result that more of your premiums could go towards the savings component of the policy and you could conceivably accumulate more wealth. Eventually, the death benefit could get quite low. My company used to allow clients to get as little as $10,000 in coverage over time, leaving the rest for investment. But because you've put in relatively high premiums, your death benefit has remained pretty high, even with the wealth-maximizer plan. It's just the way the numbers work out."

"I'm still a bit in shock," said Catherine, laughing.

"Charles, how does $15,000 a year for fifteen years grow to $1.2 million?"

"Well," I replied, "the most important factor is simple: the money has accumulated tax-deferred inside the policy. Joyce and Rob have got both the so-called miracle of compound interest *and* the bonus of deferred taxes working for them, so wealth can accumulate faster than it would in a non-tax-exempt investment."

"Of course," said Peter.

"And that $1.2 million includes the death benefit. It's payable only if Joyce dies, and we're not hoping to cash in on that option any time soon. The cash value of the policy is what Joyce and Rob can play with — they can withdraw it, use it for collateral against a loan, or let it continue to accumulate. When Joyce is sixty, assuming that the money continues to grow at an average of 9 percent a year, the cash value will be roughly half a million dollars. When she's seventy, the cash value will be around $800,000."

"Okay," said Catherine. "That makes more sense to me. But I'm still curious to know just how this policy has worked."

"Let's take a closer look," I said. "Ten years ago, Rob and Joyce take out a universal life policy on her life with a face value, or death benefit, of $500,000. The minimum amount they can pay to keep the policy in force and pay for the insurance is around $2,700 a year. The maximum amount is more like $21,000 a year. Because they're looking at this policy as an aggressive retirement savings vehicle, they want to overfund it. So they decide on a figure of fifteen grand a year for fifteen years, for a total investment of $225,000."

"I'm with you so far," said Catherine.

"Great. Now, this is a long-term strategy; the advantages of the policy begin to become evident after about five years, depending on the investment decisions you make. It gets better and better the longer you wait. In the first years, in fact, most of your premiums are going to cover the insurance company's issue costs. After year one, for example, if Joyce and Rob had decided that they'd made a mistake and wanted out, they could have cashed in the policy — but for less than $6,000. That would have been a loss of more than 50 percent on their $15,000 premium."

"The big mistake would have been cancelling the policy," said Rob.

"Exactly. I can't stress enough that you've got to see this as a long-term strategy," I said. "Let's say that the money invested grows at just 6 percent a year. After five years, when Joyce and Rob have invested $75,000, they'll only just be starting to break even — that is, the cash surrender value in the policy will be about $75,000. After ten years and $150,000 in premiums, the cash value is more like $205,000. And after fifteen years and $225,000 in premiums, you've got nearly $370,000 in cash value. At that point, the money will just continue to grow via the magic of compounding."

"Charles, how do you remember all these numbers?" said Peter.

"I did this every day for years," I reminded him. "They're pretty much etched into my brain. Also, Joyce and Rob and I did a policy review when I visited them at Christmas. So the numbers are relatively fresh in my head."

"I guess that makes sense," he said, "but I couldn't keep them all in my head."

"You get used to it," I said.

"But getting back to this 6 percent," said Catherine. "That's a relatively low rate of return, isn't it?"

"It is," I said. "In fact, Joyce and Rob have achieved more like a 9 percent overall interest rate, which is excellent, especially when you consider that almost none of that money is going to taxes, aside from provincial taxes on premiums. I always tend to use 6 percent as a figure when I'm talking about a return on investment. It's just habit; when I did insurance illustrations for clients, I liked to keep the potential rate of return low. It's always better to be on the conservative side when estimating returns. That said, however, you could do very well in a universal life policy. If you'd invested all during the boom markets in the 1990s, it would have been difficult to earn only 6 percent on your money. On the other hand, if you'd invested heavily in NASDAQ-based funds in the year 2000, you probably would have lost a lot."

"How do you invest inside a universal life policy?" asked Peter. "Can you buy stocks and mutual funds, and things like that?"

"Not quite," I replied. "As I told Andrew and Rebecca, your investment options are usually more limited. You can't buy specific stocks, although that might change in a few years. And some companies are just starting to investigate mutual funds within their UL portfolios. Right now, you can put money into things like GICs for fixed, guaranteed rates. Or you can go into index funds that follow specific stock exchanges or markets, like the Toronto Stock Exchange, money-market indices, the Standard & Poor's 500, or the good old NASDAQ. Of course, you can balance your portfolio with a mixture of investments: put 25 percent in bond indices, another 25 percent in international equities, another quarter in American equities, and the remainder in Canadian small-cap funds, if you'd like. Of course, with more choice and control over where you put your money, there's more risk."

"So you invest your money for the fifteen or twenty years, and it grows tax-deferred," said Peter. "But what happens when you want to actually spend the stuff? I mean, I'm sure that Joyce and Rob want to golf and travel lots in their retirement."

"Oh, we do," said my sister.

"Well," continued Peter, "when you withdraw the money from the policy, won't you have to pay tax on it?"

"If we actually withdrew the money from the policy, yes,

we would have to pay tax on it," said Joyce. "But we won't do that. Instead, we'll use the built-up cash value in the policy as collateral for a loan."

"We'll live off the loan and pay a relatively low interest rate to the bank rather than a high tax rate to the government," continued Rob. "And when we die, the bank is paid back through the death benefit. The kids receive whatever's left over, tax-free."

"If there *is* anything left over," added Joyce. "We might just go through everything, and we'll have a great time doing it!"

"That's very smart!" said Peter, sitting back in his chair. Peter always loves good systems.

"It is a good idea," I said. "You leverage the cash value of the policy in order to create a virtually tax-free retirement fund. What's more, if you use the loan money to buy stocks, bonds, or segregated or mutual funds, the interest on the loan could be considered tax-deductible, since you're borrowing to invest. If it's clear that you're using the money to supplement your retirement income, however, you won't be able to deduct the interest."

"And banks go along with this arrangement?" asked Catherine.

"Oh, yes," I replied. "Many insurance companies have specific agreements with banks to allow for that kind of leveraging. The banks will generally lend up to 90 percent of the cash surrender value of a policy if the funds in the policy are invested in guaranteed accounts. If you're in riskier equities, they'll usually lend up to 50 percent. So as you near the age when you'll want to leverage the money, Joyce and Rob, you may well want to switch from equities to guaranteed investments."

"How do you pay back the interest on the loan?" asked Catherine.

"The loan is capitalized, which means that the bank will lend you enough money to pay the annual interest. It adds that amount to the original loan. When the insured dies, the death benefit is used to repay the loan, including capitalized interest. The potential risk here is that you live well beyond your life expectancy. If Joyce lives to be one hundred, for example, the accumulated loans and interest might be greater than she or the bank had anticipated. In that case, the banks might ask for additional security for the loan, or perhaps for repayment or a surrender of the policy."

"Charles, this is all so tidy," said Peter. "Why aren't universal life plans more popular?"

"Actually, they're becoming quite popular," I said. "In fact, universal life policies make up something like 60 percent of all life insurance policies sold in Canada today, and that percentage is increasing. As well, people aren't taking out universal life policies simply to supplement their retirement incomes. In the past few years, I had a few clients who decided to take out UL policies on their young grandchildren."

"On their grandchildren?" said Joyce. "Since when did little kids need life insurance and retirement savings?"

"Generally, they don't," I answered, "at least not in the short run. But my clients were thinking of longer-term investing. I mean, look at your UL policy, Joyce. You and Rob have put in a substantial amount of money each year for the past decade, and you're looking at another decade or so of premiums before the investment really pays off. If you had been able to take out the same policy as a newborn, just think of how well you could have done. Starting at an early age means that you can invest a lot less money and still build a lot of wealth. That's how my clients see it. They also see it as a way to minimize taxes and probate fees on their estates."

"So how would a grandparent go about setting up such a policy?" asked Rob.

"Well, it's simple, really," I said. "Say a grandfather with a fair amount of disposable income or savings decides that he wants to make a lasting contribution to the financial well-being of his baby granddaughter. He'd like to minimize probate fees and taxes on his estate as well. He'd also like to spend some of his money now to minimize his estate later. So he applies for a universal life insurance policy, and then designates the granddaughter as the insured and someone else — usually her parents — as the beneficiary. He's the owner of the policy, and he pays the premiums."

"They can't be much for a newborn baby," said Catherine.

"Exactly," I said, "which is why this strategy can be such an effective wealth-builder for the child. Say the death benefit for the policy is somewhere in the vicinity of half a million dollars. Well, because the risk of premature death for a newborn is so low, the minimum premium for that kind of policy might be just a few hundred dollars. The maximum premium to keep the policy's tax-exempt status, however, might be something like $5,000. Well, if Granddad decides to put in $4,000 every year, that money will grow in a tax-sheltered investment account until the granddaughter withdraws it or uses it as collateral for a loan. She might use it to fund her university education. Who knows, she might decide to pull a 'Joyce and Rob,' and not touch the money until she retires. But if she does decide to withdraw money from the policy as a student, she'll probably pay tax on the withdrawal at a much lower rate than her parents or her grandfather would."

"And when Grandpa dies, the policy goes to the granddaughter, tax-free, right?" asked Peter.

"Yes, that's one possibility," I said, "as long as that's what he's specified in his will. Or he might decide at some point before he dies to transfer ownership to his granddaughter, say right before she goes to university or decides to buy a house. If he dies while she's too young to handle the policy, Grandpa can stipulate a contingent owner, such as the girl's parents, to manage the policy until she's old enough."

"So what kind of growth potential are we looking at?" asked Rob.

"Well, let's keep going with the example above, which actually is what one of my clients decided to do for his granddaughter. I did up the illustration for him. He bought a $475,000 policy on the baby, and he's going to put in $4,000 a year for twenty years. If the investment returns even a conservative 6 percent, his granddaughter will have access to cash value of just over $125,000 by the time she's nineteen. Her total death benefit will be close to a million dollars — $925,000 and change, to be exact."

"Not bad," said Joyce.

"Not at all," I said. "Now, just imagine that the baby's proud parents have contributed to RESPs her whole life, so she doesn't need to withdraw funds from the policy for university. She just leaves the money in the policy untouched until she's fifty years old. Her grandfather has long since passed away, but he's left her a tax-sheltered legacy in the policy. At that point, the cash value will be in the neighbourhood of $890,000, and the total death benefit will be nearly $2.3 million! And that's a conservative investment."

"And then she can think about doing what Joyce and Rob have done," said Catherine, "and use that money to supplement her retirement savings."

"Precisely," I said. "The other great thing about this policy is that the granddaughter has never had to worry about buying — or qualifying for — life insurance. Because the policy was overfunded early on, it's generated enough in the way of interest or investment earnings to pay for the insurance portion. So Grandpa has given her two gifts in one."

"Very nice," said Peter. "How many grandchildren does your client have, Charles?"

"Only the one," I said. "It's considerably easier to do it for one than it would be to do for five!"

"Charles," said Catherine, "I don't mean to be macabre, but wouldn't an insurance company be a little . . . worried about such a large death benefit for a newborn? What about foul play — you know, all those tabloid magazine stories about children being killed for large insurance payouts?"

"Yes, we've all heard of those," I said. "That kind of case is rare, but it happens. For this kind of policy, the insurer will require that the parents are adequately insured. It also may require the parents to co-sign the application. And of course, the child must be healthy. For any large policy issued on a child's life, the insurance company will investigate to make sure that the intentions are honourable."

"You know," said Rob, "I sometimes wonder how the government — specifically, the taxman — can allow these policies to exist. Universal life seems like such a good deal that I'm surprised the government doesn't want to take a share of the profits."

"That's a really good point, Rob," I said. "There's always the possibility of the government changing the tax rules. Right now, leveraging a UL policy is so attractive because of the favourable tax rules: there's no tax on life insurance proceeds, no tax on the funds that accumulate in the policies, and no tax on the loans or the cash value as collateral."

"What's the likelihood that the rules will change?" asked Joyce.

"Who knows?" I said. "In theory, the government is free to change the rules at any time. But I don't think that it will. I can't imagine the general public would react too kindly to finding out that life insurance proceeds were now taxable, for example. And it seems to me that if the folks at the Department of Finance decide to tax the cash value of a UL policy when it's used as collateral, they'd be in trouble again."

"Why?" asked Rob.

"Well, in today's financial markets, billions of dollars in property are already used as collateral. People and businesses mortgage houses and buildings and other savings all the time, for example. So if the government decided to tax the cash value used as collateral, it would in fairness have to tax all the other property used for the same purpose, and that would wreak havoc in the economy and marketplace. It would be pretty drastic. The good news is that even if it did change the rules, the government would probably protect existing UL leveraging arrangements with transitional rules. You know, a grandfather clause of some kind."

"What about anti-avoidance legislation?" asked Rob.

"What's that?" Joyce asked her husband.

"Oh, the GAAR, or general anti-avoidance rule. It's a way for the Canada Customs and Revenue Agency to make sure that people aren't abusing the tax system," he replied.

"The GAAR also is a concern," I said. "But again, if other laws make clear that using the cash value as collateral is perfectly acceptable, I don't see how it's an abuse. Just because you choose to use the tax strategies legally available to you doesn't mean that you're abusing the system. In my opinion, the GAAR isn't going to be contravened here. Of course, I could be wrong about all of this, but lots of experts feel the same way. Think of it like this: governments are capable of changing the rules for every investment opportunity out there. That shouldn't stop you from investing."

"True," said Peter, getting up. "Can I get anyone a drink?"

"Hey, Peter," I said, "weren't you going to get out the good Scotch?"

"That," he said, "is for *after* dinner. I will be back in a moment."

Peter retreated into the cottage and returned in record time with a bottle of white wine.

"Charles," he said, holding the bottle by its neck as he spoke, "I just had a thought: I'm turning sixty-nine this year, so I have to wind up my RRSP by December. We've been talking about retirement income strategies all evening, and it just occurred to me that you might well have some life insurance tricks up your sleeve when it comes to retirement. I think it's time for my own insurance seminar. Any suggestions?"

"I'd love to talk about this, but my throat's a little dry," I said, looking meaningfully towards the wine.

Peter laughed, then handed around glasses and poured. I took a sip.

"There are a few life insurance tricks in terms of retirement income," I said. "They tend to focus on protecting the value of your estate while deferring or reducing taxes. I can let you in on a couple of secrets, though."

"I'd appreciate it," he said.

"Well, I guess the first thing to know is that you have three options when it comes to winding up your RRSP. You already know that you have to choose one of them by the end of the year, so it's a good idea to start thinking about those options now."

"What are they?" asked Joyce.

"Well, the first one isn't really an option: you could just withdraw all the money from your RRSP and pay a hefty tax bill. Unless you know you've got a year to live and want to make the most of it, I wouldn't recommend going this route."

"My goodness, it's sometimes tempting, though," said Catherine. "All those years of savings, and every so often I want to just blow it all!"

"Don't we all," I said. "But the gods of practicality and tax efficiency usually take over, and they dictate that the two sane RRSP strategies are to buy an annuity or transfer the money into a RRIF, or registered retirement income fund. Personally, I tend to favour the latter."

"Why?" asked Catherine.

"Well, I like RRIFs because you can control your investments, just as you would with an RRSP. In fact, RRIFs are pretty similar to RRSPs, except for the fact that you can't contribute to a RRIF and you have to withdraw a certain minimum amount of money each year. But the money inside the RRIF grows tax-free until it's withdrawn, and it could potentially earn more for you than you would get by going with an annuity, where the monthly payment is fixed. And when you die, you can leave the remainder of your RRIF to your heirs. That's not an option with all annuities."

"Annuities have something to do with life insurance, don't they?" said Joyce.

"Well, they can," I answered. "Buying an annuity means that you enter into a contract, very often with a life insurance company. You pay the company a sum of money, and in return it agrees to pay you an amount each month or year, usually for a fixed period of time, or for life. You pay tax on the annuity payments you receive. For the purposes of this discussion, there are two kinds of annuities: non-prescribed and prescribed. Non-prescribed annuities are purchased with registered funds — like the money in your RRSP. Prescribed annuities are purchased with non-registered money — pretty much anything *outside* an RRSP. Are you with me so far?"

"Crystal clear," said Joyce.

"Good. Now, there is a strategy, called a back-to-back prescribed annuity, that uses life insurance."

"Back-to-back," said Rob. "You buy an annuity and then an insurance policy, one after the other?"

"Exactly," I said. "Take the example of a retiree who has a lot of interest-bearing investments, like GICs. The interest on these kinds of investments is taxed as income, at your highest rate. If you had $100,000 in GICs, and you earned 6.5 percent interest on them, you'd have $6,500 in taxable income. If you had other investments and income, you might be in a 50 percent tax bracket, so you'd be left with $3,250 after taxes. The advantage, however, would be that you'd hold on to the original $100,000, which you could eventually leave to the kids or spend.

"Now," I continued, "you could take your $100,000 and buy an annuity that paid something like $12,000 a year. Well, only part of that annuity payment is taxable, so you'd end up with more money, even after taxes, than you would have by living on the GIC interest alone, maybe $10,000, which is a big improvement."

"I'll say," said Joyce. "I'd take $10,000 over $3,250 any day."

"Me too," I said. "The only problem is that you can no longer rely on holding on to your hundred thousand — it's gone into the annuity. So what will you leave to the kids?"

"Let me guess," said Catherine. "You use some of the extra money you got from the annuity to buy a life insurance policy with a death benefit of $100,000. When you die, that goes to the kids!"

"Bingo," I said. "As long as the cost of the premiums doesn't cancel out the tax savings, you've come out ahead. While you're at it, you could consider investing some of your extra cash in vehicles that have a better rate of return than your annuity. Nowadays, with universal life, most companies will issue policies until you're eighty, if you're in good health. So say you're sixty-nine or seventy, and it's time to collapse your RRSP. Well, you've also potentially got a pension from your company and the Canada Pension Plan, Old Age Security, and maybe other income if you sell your house to move somewhere smaller. You might find that you have more income than you need. Why not shelter it by taking out a UL policy? You can build wealth and minimize taxes, and when you die, the tax-free benefit goes to the next generation."

My stomach rumbled, as if to punctuate that last remark. We all laughed.

"That's about all that's in my bag of tricks for RRSP rollovers," I said. "There are a lot of post-retirement and estate-planning life insurance tricks, but we can talk about them on a full stomach. Anyone else hungry?" I asked.

"Starving, actually," said Rob.

Joyce nodded emphatically.

"Yes, let's fire up the barbecue and eat," said Catherine.

RECIPES FOR SUCCESS

1 Properly funded and maintained, universal life insurance can be a great way to provide extra income during your retirement. But remember: UL is a long-term strategy.

2 Generally, money in UL plans can be invested in GICs or index funds, which follow the ups and downs of various stock exchanges and markets, like the Standard & Poor's 500 or the NASDAQ. You can balance your portfolio with a mixture of eligible investments.

3 The cash value inside a UL plan grows tax-deferred until it's withdrawn. To minimize the tax hit, however, you can leverage the funds inside the plan. Many banks will give loans of up to 90 percent of the policy's cash value, using the money inside the policy as collateral. You pay interest on the loan but continue to defer taxes! Upon your death, the bank receives the death benefit to pay back the loan.

4 Grandparents looking to make a substantial gift to their grandchildren can buy UL policies for them.

5 A back-to-back prescribed annuity involves buying an annuity *and* a life insurance policy. With the tax savings generated from your annuity, you can buy a policy that pays a death benefit to your beneficiaries.

9

You Can't Take It with You:

Joint Last-to-Die, Long-Term Care, Guaranteed Issue, and Planned Giving

Whenever the senior members of the Stonehouse clan get together, you can be sure of two things: golf and good food. On Sunday morning, Peter, Joyce, Rob, and I drove to the nearby Mont Ste. Marie golf course to play eighteen holes. Catherine volunteered to go to town and do some grocery shopping in preparation for that night's dinner, which promised to be nothing short of fantastic.

Of course, when it comes to golf, Peter and I aren't at all competitive — at least, we don't think we are, although Catherine might have something different to say on the subject. In any case, neither of us can beat Joyce or Rob, who play at their golf club in Markham, Ontario, as often as their busy work schedules will allow. I like to think that their relative youth gives them a comparative advantage over Peter and me. Wishful thinking, I'm sure, although there is one advantage to getting older when you play golf: with each passing year, it becomes easier to score your age!

After the game, we had lunch and a cold beer at the clubhouse. I had scored a respectable 97, and Peter had done slightly better, coming in at 95. I would have bested him,

I muttered good-naturedly, had I not lost my ball on the eighteenth hole. Joyce and Rob, as usual, played brilliantly: he came in at 85, and my little sister at 91.

Over lunch, talk turned to our plans for dinner. We were going to create a Thai feast that evening — Peter and Catherine had taken a month-long trip to Thailand for their fortieth anniversary a few years back, and they had come home raving not only about the people and the sights, but also the fantastic food. Tonight's menu would consist of green mango salad, pad Thai with shrimp, spicy mussels, and chicken and shrimp satays done on the barbecue. Lime and mango sherbet for dessert. As we ate, we crafted our master plan of attack: Catherine would make the pad Thai, her specialty; Peter would cook the mussels; Rob would bartend and man the barbecue; Joyce was in charge of the mango salad; and I was responsible for the rice. For a change, the bread-maker would play no role in this cottage meal!

◆ ◆ ◆

"Oh," groaned Joyce. "I can't believe we ate all that!"

The rest of us nodded, too full, for the time being, to say much. We sat outside on the deck, nursing our glasses of wine and watching the remainder of the sunset. It was a perfect cottage evening — we could hear the chirping of crickets and the occasional call of a bird. Peter had lit citronella torches, keeping the mosquitoes at bay. Good company, good food, a beautiful setting . . . once again, I reflected on how lucky I had been to spend my first retirement summer at the cottage.

Obviously, my siblings and their partners were having similar thoughts.

"This is just beautiful," said Joyce to Peter and Catherine. "I can't tell you how great it is to be up here and spend time with all of you. We don't do this nearly often enough."

"Perhaps now that we're all hitting retirement age, we'll do it more," I said. "I mean, I never had the luxury of the entire summer off when I worked."

"That's true," said Catherine, picking at a bit of mango salad. "I have to say, I've really enjoyed the whole summer. Having Charles up here, and being able to see all my children and grandchildren, and now Joyce and Rob — I couldn't have chosen a better arrangement. I feel as though this cottage has really become the hub of family life."

"How long have you two owned it?" asked Rob.

"It's been in my family for generations," answered Catherine. She sounded a bit wistful. "You know, I think my grandfather bought this property for less than a thousand dollars. And I love seeing the kids, and their kids, enjoy it. I wonder if Granddad knew what an important investment he had made."

"I imagine he had some idea," mused Rob. "I'm sure he'd be thrilled to know that his great-great-grandchildren were still running around the place, having a blast."

"I wonder how many more generations of your family will spend their summers here, Catherine," said Joyce.

"Well, if I have my way, this cottage will stay in our family for a good long time," answered Catherine. "The kids know that's what we want. With Charles's advice, Peter and I have ensured that it'll go equally to all four children, and that they won't have to pay the disposition taxes on it."

"How did you manage that?" asked Rob.

"Well, it's no secret that this property is worth a lot of money. As you can imagine, its value has risen substantially since my grandfather bought it! We want to leave it to all four children in our wills, but we know they're going to be hit with a large tax bill for capital gains when they get it. And because they're all in different places financially, I'd hate to see any of them strapped for cash trying to pay the taxes — or having to sell their shares to each other or, worse, to a stranger. So Peter and I have an insurance policy — what's it called, Charles?"

"A joint last-to-die policy," I said.

"Yes, a joint last-to-die policy that pays out after we both die. If I die first, for example, everything goes to Peter, tax-free — you know, the spousal rollover?"

"Actually," I interjected, "it's not quite that the property goes to the spouse tax-free, but rather that the tax is deferred. In other words, when the first spouse in a couple dies, all the assets are transferred to the surviving spouse and the taxes deferred until his or her death. When the second spouse dies, the assets are taxed as though they had been sold at fair market value. In the case of this cottage, that could be a lot of capital gains tax for the kids to pay."

"Thanks, Charles," said Catherine. "And that tax bill worried us. So the insurance policy we have pays out only upon the death of the second spouse. At that point, the death benefit will be enough to cover the taxes on the cottage so that the kids can inherit it without the tax burden."

"Very smart!" said Rob approvingly. "Charles, you were the mastermind of this plan?"

"Of course," I said modestly. "Actually, it's a pretty common tax strategy. People often use life insurance as a way of offsetting the taxes owing upon death. Say, for the sake of easy math, that this cottage has appreciated by $400,000 since Catherine inherited it. Well, 50 percent of the capital gain will be brought into the estate to be taxed. So when the kids inherit the cottage, at a 50 percent marginal tax rate, they'll end up owing a collective $100,000 or so in tax. So Peter and Catherine take out a joint last-to-die, term-to-100 or universal life policy with a $100,000 death benefit, with the kids as the joint beneficiaries. With the death of the second spouse, the policy pays out the death benefit to the kids, who use the money to pay the capital gains taxes. And — voilà! — the cottage stays in the family, and no one child is forced to go into debt or sell his or her share."

"So you both have to die before the death benefit becomes payable," said Joyce, nodding slowly. "That would also be a good policy for two people who were otherwise self-insured, wouldn't it?"

"What do you mean?" I asked.

"Well, say you had a family with kids and two spouses who both earned a lot of money in their respective careers," said Joyce. "If one spouse died, the other might very well be able to carry on supporting the kids on one income, and vice versa. But if both spouses died, then those kids could be in a lot of trouble. So wouldn't their parents need a joint last-to-die policy that paid out only when the second spouse passed away?"

"Yes," I said. "Very good point. Over the years, I've had a few clients where that was the case. That's a great use for joint last-to-die policies. But the big market for this type of plan is folks like Peter and Catherine, who use it as part of an estate plan. And that market is growing. You've heard the phrase 'the trillion-dollar generation'?"

"Ah, yes," said Peter. "The baby boomers! They're going to inherit a trillion dollars in the next decades!"

"Right," I said, "and the Canadian government is thrilled about this, because they're going to collect a very large chunk of that trillion bucks in the form of income taxes upon death. Naturally, boomers will be loath to watch half of their inheritance go to the taxman. So they're beginning to see that life insurance is a great way to minimize the tax bite."

"So you pay less in premiums than you would in taxes?" asked Rob.

"Generally, yes," I replied. "Otherwise, it wouldn't be worth the bother. First of all, joint last-to-die policies tend to be less expensive than regular polices because two people are insured under one. For pricing purposes, the insurance company converts the ages of the two people into the equivalent single-life age: a sixty-eight-year-old man and a sixty-five-year-old woman, both non-smokers, might be insured for the price of one fifty-four-year-old. So you save some cash right there."

"Wow, Rob," said Joyce, "when you add up our ages, we become younger. Wonderful!"

"Well, only in the eyes of the insurance company, unfortunately," I said. "But, Rob, to continue answering your question, you'd almost always pay less in premiums than you would get in benefits. Let's take any old example. Say Peter and Catherine take out a joint last-to-die term-to-100 or universal life policy with a death benefit of $200,000. And say the premiums on that policy are $4,000 a year and the second death takes place in twenty years. During that time, they've put in $80,000. Well, for that investment, their beneficiaries receive, tax-free, the $200,000, a gain of $120,000. It actually works out to an annual return of something like 8.8 percent, tax-free! That's not a bad investment."

"Not at all," said Rob. "And it's safer than a whole lot of other investments, unless Peter and Catherine live into their late nineties, or even to one hundred."

"That's the tricky part," I said. "We can't predict with any accuracy when we're going to die."

"You know, I understand why you want to make sure that the cottage stays in the family, Catherine," said Joyce. "And I think that if I owned a similar property, I might be inspired to do the same kind of thing. But I guess I've never given much thought to what the kids will inherit. I just assume that we'll leave them whatever we leave them, and they can pay the taxes on it themselves."

"That's understandable, Joyce," I said. "It's a very personal financial choice. I had lots of clients who felt as you do, and rightly so. As they say, you can't take it with you. Why pay a lot of money every year to save on taxes *after* your death, when those savings won't benefit you?"

"Exactly," said my sister. "I just don't see the point. I mean, I have no desire to burden my sons with hefty tax bills, but I'm sure they'll be just fine paying out some of their inheritance to the taxman. That's life — or death, in this case."

"I have one suggestion for you, though," I told my sister. "If *you* don't want to pay the premiums on life insurance that you won't need, why not give Spencer and Fraser the option of paying the premiums for a joint last-to-die policy on you and Rob? They don't have to take it out now, but they might want to think about it in five or ten years. It could be a worthwhile investment for them — you know, that 8.8 percent return, tax-free."

"You've got a point," said Joyce. "If they're going to be stuck paying the taxes at some point in the future, maybe they'll want to plan for it now and pay less over the long run. You know, that may not be such a bad idea. Rob, why don't we talk to Spence and Fraser about it when we get home? They can make the final decision."

"Sound fine to me," said her husband. "I have the feeling, though, that Spencer will think it's a great idea and Fraser won't."

"In that case," I said, "there's nothing preventing Spencer from taking out — and paying the premiums on — a term-to-100 policy on your lives for half the expected tax liability."

"Good point," said Rob. "There's no reason they both have to do it."

"I can see the merits of insuring against future taxes, Charles," said Joyce. "And I'd be happy if the boys wanted to go ahead and do that — or not, for that matter. What I *really* worry about, though, isn't that they'll have to pay taxes on a generous inheritance — it's that they'll have to take care of Robert and me in our old age, and they'll wipe out their own savings, as well as our assets. I guess my insurance priority has always been to make sure that we'll have enough so that our sons won't be burdened — emotionally or financially — by caring for us. That's one reason I'm happy with what we've done with the UL policy we have. I mean, Rob's dad died of Alzheimer's, and I don't know what we would have done at the end without twenty-four-hour care. I don't want to put Spencer or Fraser through the ordeal of caring for us without any help."

"It's not only emotionally and physically draining, it's expensive," added Rob, putting down his wine glass. "I mean, take a look at Stuart, one of my partners. Now, he's in a tricky situation, one that I certainly don't want our kids ever to face. You know how I just mentioned the possibility that we could live into our nineties? Well, Stuart is living a version of that story. He's sixty-five, and his mother-in-law is ninety-one years old and going strong. He loves her to bits, but she needs round-the-clock-care, and he and his wife are paying an arm and a leg to keep her in a good nursing home. I think the fees are something like $2,300 a month. Her Old Age Security covers part of that, but the proceeds from the sale of her house and all her savings were exhausted a few years ago, so Stuart is covering the bulk of the costs. They actually had to dip into his wife's RRSPs this year to cover them. And he's retiring soon, which means he'll be supporting her through his retirement income. He's got three kids, one of whom is still in university, and they're paying for that, too. He's exhausted and worried. I don't think he ever imagined that he'd be paying for a parent's nursing home expenses in his own retirement, but that's what's happened."

"What an awful situation," said Catherine, shaking her head. "But you know, I suppose that as our population ages, it's bound to become more common. People will want to make sure their ageing parents receive the proper care, even if it ends up bankrupting them."

"Or people will find themselves taking care of their own spouses," Rob pointed out.

"Often getting sick themselves in the process," said Joyce. "I've had patients like that."

"And then there are cases when the ageing parent goes to live with one of the kids," said Peter. "If Mom or Dad gets sick or infirm, the kids have to take care of them or hire someone to help out. That can be just as financially and emotionally draining as putting a parent into a nursing home, I imagine."

"And parents don't want to be a burden," added Joyce. "But in some cases, there's no choice. I mean, I'm sure that Stuart's mother-in-law never imagined that she would live into her nineties, or that her children would find themselves strapped for cash because of it. She and her husband saved all their lives, and it still wasn't enough."

"I hate to tell you this, but there are going to be a lot more 'Stuarts' out there in the next couple of decades," I said. "Just have a look at the demographics. I recently read a Statistics Canada report that said that Canadians eighty-five and older are the fastest-growing segment of the senior population. This is a hot topic — a lot of parents and children are going to be looking for solutions to the problem of caring for elderly parents."

"That's exactly what we've been investigating, Charles," said Joyce. "Actually, I meant to talk to you about the option of long-term-care insurance."

"Ah, yes," I said, reaching for the bottle opener. "That's another area of the insurance market that's getting a lot of attention as the boomers begin to retire, and their parents begin to need more care." I uncorked another bottle of wine and refreshed our glasses as the conversation continued. Joyce and Rob had brought a couple of great bottles from the Niagara region.

"What's long-term-care insurance?" asked Peter.

"Pretty much exactly what it sounds like, isn't it, Charles?" said Rob. "It's insurance that will cover the costs of caring for you in your old age — if you no longer can."

"Yes," continued Joyce. "So it'll cover the out-of-pocket costs for a nursing home — or even home care, if you need someone to come into your home but don't need or want to go into a nursing home just yet."

"How does it work?" asked Catherine. "I mean, how does the insurance company decide when it's appropriate to pay? Do you just check into the nursing home?"

"No," I said, "it's not quite that simple. Usually, the payments are designed to kick in when and if the insured can no longer independently perform two or more activities of daily living. So if the insured could no longer dress and feed him- or herself, that would count. Generally, the insured would be assessed by a doctor, who would certify to the company that he or she needed long-term care."

"Can anybody get coverage?" asked Rob.

"Well, generally, the insurance company will want to know about your current health before they'll issue a policy," I said. "If you're already in a nursing home or need help with everyday tasks of daily living, it's doubtful that they'll approve you for a policy. They'll probably want to know about how well you function cognitively, your general health, the medications you take, why and how often you've seen your doctor recently, and your family medical history. And of course, if you're too old — usually eighty and up — you won't qualify at all."

"I imagine that kind of coverage would be quite costly," said Peter. "After all, private nurses and good nursing homes are expensive, aren't they? I mean, look at what your friend Stuart is paying every month for his mother-in-law."

"You're right," I said, "the premiums for long-term-care coverage aren't cheap — they can cost more than $2,000 a year. The older you get, obviously, the more expensive the policy will be. And some insurers will charge higher fees for women, because women have a longer life expectancy. "

"Ouch," said Peter.

"Yup — the premiums are no walk in the park. But you have to weigh the costs of the insurance against the costs of the care itself — and the likelihood that you'll need it. A few thousand dollars is a drop in the bucket compared with the costs of keeping an elderly person in a good home or paying for home care. I read an article recently that said the average stay in a *subsidized* nursing-care facility is a little longer than two and a half years and could cost $100,000 in Ontario. As people live longer and longer, the probability of being institutionalized increases. I mean, look at life expectancy. Today, a sixty-five-year-old man can expect to live to the age of nearly eighty-four, and a woman of the same age can expect to live until eighty-seven. And I read an article recently that said that almost 40 percent of women and 25 percent of men over the age of eighty-five live in institutions."

"It's a bit scary, isn't it?" said Joyce. "It scares me to death. I'd much rather pay the premiums than find myself needing care and unable to pay for it. Of course, I think I'm still a bit young to be buying the coverage, but it's on our agenda."

"One good thing about some LTC plans — that's what they're called, by the way, by those of us 'in the know' — is that they have a couple of features that make the premiums a little easier to take," I said. "Not much, but a little. There are riders that waive premiums while you're receiving benefits, for example. So if you check into a nursing home, you no longer have to pay the premiums that keep you there. There's also a 'limited premium payment period' rider, which means that you might have to pay premiums only until a certain age or for a certain amount of time — usually twenty years or until age sixty-five or eighty-five, for example. After that, the policy is considered paid up. It's comforting because at least you know that you won't be stuck paying premiums into your nineties or hundreds. Also, some policies have a non-forfeiture benefit: if you stop paying premiums, they'll reduce your benefits, but they won't cancel the policy outright, at least not immediately."

"What if you die without needing the benefits?" asked Catherine. "Will they refund your premiums, the way they will with some disability policies if you don't make a claim?"

"Yes, a return-of-premium rider, which is what you're talking about, is certainly available for many policies. In some cases, the policy must have been in force for more than five years, and must still be in force at time of death, for the rider to apply."

"So all you risk, really, is the opportunity cost," said Peter, "the potential loss of the income that your money could have generated if you'd invested it elsewhere."

"Exactly," I said. "Mind you, that's nothing to sneeze at. Invest $2,000 a year for twenty years, and you'll potentially earn a lot. Just look at Joyce and Rob's universal life policy."

"True," he said. "That *is* quite the savings plan."

"Charles, can you get a policy with premiums that are guaranteed not to go up, like you can with disability insurance?" asked Catherine.

"Some companies have them," I said. "Others will guarantee premiums for five years. Usually, however, they can raise your premiums only if they're raising rates across the board. Actually, disability and long-term-care policies have some basic features in common, although they're designed for different purposes. For example, you can choose your elimination period for both kinds of policies. For LTC, it's generally zero, sixty, or ninety days. And you can also choose the benefit period, which is usually one, two, or five years, or lifetime. The shorter the elimination period and the longer the benefit period, the more expensive the policy. You can also build in extra coverage as inflation rates rise."

"How much coverage can you get?" asked Peter.

"Generally, you choose the amount of coverage you apply for," I said. "Sometimes companies offer a flat benefit for a certain rate. As we've discussed, the cost would be based on the age and health status of the insured, the elimination and benefit periods chosen, the riders you add to the policy, and the type of coverage specified — for example, do you want both home care *and* institutional care? The premium costs go up pretty dramatically as you enter your late sixties and seventies. Most policies have a cut-off point of about age seventy-five or eighty, when they'll no longer issue LTC insurance."

"I wonder," said Peter, "do some people buy this type of coverage when they're relatively young and it's relatively inexpensive? I mean, if a forty-year-old bought LTC insurance, he'd have to pay for only twenty years, and he could get that return-of-premium rider if he never used the benefits."

"I'm sure that some people have done exactly that," I said. "Mostly, however, people in their forties find that they have more pressing expenses than pre-paying LTC insurance, like paying off the mortgage and educating the kids. Or figuring out what to do about their own ageing parents. If you were incredibly forward-thinking, perhaps you'd choose LTC coverage in your forties. But I don't have many clients who have done that. On the other hand, it's a relatively new product, so it just might be that in the future, people will begin to save for their long-term care the way they do for their retirements."

"We're only just starting to think about it now," said Joyce. "I read a newspaper article about it a few weeks ago and thought I'd ask you about it when we got here."

"Well, it's a great product if you need it and can afford it," I said. "But the word 'need' is key. In your case, Joyce, I'd be surprised if you and Rob need to insure against the possibility that you'll need care and won't be able to afford it. I mean, there's no doubt that home care and nursing homes are expensive, but with all the planning you and Rob have done with your universal life policy and RRSPs, as well as your other savings and investments, I'm sure you could easily cover the costs of any care you might need later in life."

"You're probably right," said my sister. "You know, I guess with reading all the literature and seeing my share of elderly patients, I get a little worried."

"You'll be fine," I said.

"Charles," said Rob, "if Joyce and I are capable of overinsuring ourselves, what about people who don't have any coverage? I mean, look at . . . Joyce, who's your friend whose aunt died?"

"Oh, right," said Joyce. "Carol. She's a therapist in my office building. Her great-aunt died last year, at the age of eighty-three, and they found out rather quickly that she had no life insurance and no savings. She was living in a rented apartment. Carol had to write a cheque for $10,000 to the funeral home while the family scrambled to get her aunt's finances in order. In the end, the funeral cost about $15,000, and the family had to cover most of that themselves. I kept wondering what they could have done instead."

"Well, there are government death benefits, but the maximum there is about $2,500, and they don't kick in right away," I replied slowly. "You have to apply for them. I suppose there's always guaranteed issue."

"What's that?" asked Joyce.

"Oh, you've all seen the commercials for it," I said. "You know, the one where the phone rings and the older man grabs it and says to his wife, 'It's Patrick! He took out life insurance!' Meanwhile, good old Patrick hasn't even had the time to say, 'Hi, Dad!'"

"Oh, right!" said Catherine, laughing. "And the wife holds up the sign asking if Patrick needed to have a medical exam to qualify!"

"That's the one," I said. "Well, the life insurance they're advertising is guaranteed issue. And funny commercials aside, it's actually a popular product in Canada. It does fulfil a specific need for Canadians who can't or don't want to get any other kind of coverage: it provides an instant estate to cover final expenses, like your funeral and any last debts. That's what people usually want it for."

"So how does it work?" asked Rob. "I always wondered about those ads. It all seemed a bit suspect to me."

"It's not suspect at all. Essentially, it's just very expensive whole-life insurance," I said. "You can usually choose a death benefit of somewhere between $5,000 and $25,000. And the 'guaranteed' in 'guaranteed issue' means that almost anyone can get it, without a medical exam, which is what Patrick's mom wants to know with that sign. In my experience, that was a big selling point because there are a lot of seniors who don't want to take the time to have a medical exam or aren't anxious to know its outcome. I think that as long as you don't have cancer or HIV, aren't in a nursing home, and aren't infirm, you'll qualify."

"Why wouldn't you just buy term insurance?" asked Catherine.

"Well, you might be too old. Contrary to the commercial, where our boy Patrick is probably in his forties, guaranteed issue is usually targeted at people in their middle to late sixties who don't qualify for most other insurance policies. Or as I said, some people, including a lot of seniors, don't want to take a medical exam to qualify for cheaper term coverage. Yes, they could have bought term insurance years ago, for less money and much higher death benefits, but they didn't, for any number of reasons. And guaranteed issue becomes one of the few options left available."

"So if you're on your deathbed, you can buy this guaranteed issue over the phone and create an instant estate?" asked Rob.

"Not quite," I said. "If you die within two years of taking out the policy, the insurance company will generally pay you back only the premiums you've paid plus interest. You have to have the policy in place for two years before it'll pay the death benefit for anything other than an accidental death. That's the insurer's way of guarding against those deathbed applicants."

"How expensive is it?" asked Joyce.

"Well, if I remember correctly, the cost per thousand dollars of insurance for, say, a sixty-five-year-old non-smoking male was something like a hundred dollars."

"So premiums for $25,000 would cost $2,500 a year!" said Rob. "That's no bargain!"

"Not at all," I said. "Sometimes, however, if you really need a small amount of life insurance, guaranteed issue is your only option. Probably a better idea would have been to have planned a bit earlier, perhaps become self-insured. Even if Carol's great-aunt didn't have any dependants, she obviously could have used some kind of life insurance planning."

"Spoken like a true insurance salesman," said Peter, laughing. "You know, sometimes I can't get over the fact that Charles, our summer insurance guru, doesn't even have a life insurance policy!"

"Actually," I said, "I might have fudged a bit, just to make a point to Lindsay. I do have a life insurance policy."

"Really?" said Catherine. "But why? I mean, with your good financial planning, and Anne gone . . ."

"Well, that's exactly it," I replied. "I have a life insurance policy, and the beneficiary is the Canadian Cancer Society. I took it out right after Anne died; we had discussed it beforehand, and we wanted to be able to make a significant contribution to cancer research. So I took out a policy on my life and donated it to the society. Each year, I give them a cheque to cover the cost of the premiums, which they then pay. I get a tax receipt for the premiums. When I die, the cancer society receives the death benefit, which is sizeable.

This way, I'm able to give them much more than I would otherwise."

"What a lovely idea!" said Joyce. "I mean, we give a fair amount to different causes every year, but I've never thought about taking out a charitable life insurance policy."

"Well, it's a good way to be able to make a sizeable donation," I said. "And recent changes in tax laws make it even easier to do. The added bonus is that you — or your heirs — can save a lot of tax in the process."

"How so?" said my sister, obviously intrigued.

"Well, there are generally three ways to leave money to a charity with life insurance. First, you can transfer ownership of an existing policy to the charity. That's what some of my clients have done with older permanent policies that they no longer needed to protect their dependants. Often, the policies have been fully paid up. If you donate the policy, you get a donation receipt for any built-up cash value in the policy. And then, when you die, the charity receives the death benefit. In the meantime, however, the charity has been able to use the cash value during your lifetime, through policy loans and the like. Generally, charities would rather receive donations of permanent, as opposed to term, policies for this reason: they can access the built-up cash value before they receive the death benefit."

"What if the policy isn't fully paid up?" asked Catherine.

"Not a problem. You can still donate it, and then you'd get donation credits for the cash value and any premiums you paid *after* the donation," I replied. "Essentially, you'd write a cheque to the charity each year to cover the costs of the premiums, and the charity would issue you a donation tax receipt. You might have to pay some taxes on the cash surrender value of the policy when you transfer it, but the tax credit will usually make up for it.

"Anyway, that's the first way you can leave a policy to charity. If you donate the policy to charity, however, you won't receive any tax credits for the death benefit when it's paid out to the charity. That's where the second method comes in: buy an insurance policy in the amount you want, leave it to your estate, and then leave instructions in your will to have the death benefit donated to the good cause of your choice. This used to be the best way to do it, in my opinion, because the donation generated a donation credit that could be used to offset capital gains taxes. The problem was that by making the estate the beneficiary of the policy, you exposed the death benefit to creditors, probate, and the possibility that your will could be contested. Just imagine — your squabbling family could hold up the will forever, and your charity would never receive the donation!"

"Wasn't it Benjamin Franklin who said that if you wanted to see a person's true character, you should try to share an inheritance with them?" said Catherine. "Yes, I could see how that option could have its flaws. So what's the new, better way?"

"Well, it's what I did: take out a policy and make the charity the beneficiary. With this option, upon my death, the cancer society receives the death benefit. Great. And my estate will receive a donation credit that can offset taxes. Even better."

"By how much? This is fuzzy," said Rob.

"Well, let's plug in some real live numbers. Say that Patrick from our commercial had done a better job of life insurance planning. By the time he's our age, he's become self-insured: maybe he has a UL policy that's netted him substantial wealth, like someone else we know."

"Ha, ha," said Joyce.

"Anyway, say that upon Patrick's death, the taxable part of his estate is worth $100,000. Well, half of that gain, or $50,000, is taxable as income after his death. At a 50 percent tax bracket, his estate will owe half of that $50,000, or $25,000, in taxes. Are you with me so far?"

"Gotcha," said Rob.

"Well, say Patrick has also taken out a charitable life insurance policy for $50,000, payable to the Canadian Cancer Society. His estate gets a charitable donation receipt for $50,000. Since the donation receipt will also be taxed at 50 percent, it will generate a tax credit of $25,000 —"

"Exactly the same amount the estate has to pay in income tax!" Rob finished my sentence. "Beautiful!"

"It is beautiful," I said. "But as with many beautiful systems, there's a catch. As of the 2000 federal budget, the charitable donation you can claim is limited to 100 percent of your net income in the year of death. That's still a big increase from the former limit of 20 percent, though. So if Patrick earned $100,000 in the year he died, this strategy would work just fine. If he earned less than that, his estate could carry back the donation credit to the year before death and claim some back taxes."

"So if you earn $100,000 in the year you die, your estate can donate up to $100,000 to charity and receive the full charitable tax deduction," said Peter.

"Yes, and you can stretch any amount over the hundred grand back one more year," I said.

"But how many people in their sixties and seventies earn that much in a year?" asked Peter.

"That's the other drawback," I answered. "Not many. But still, if you'd like to make a substantial donation to a charity, and get some tax relief, life insurance is a very good option. In fact, it might be the only way that you can do it."

"Rob and Charles," said Joyce excitedly, "I just thought of a plan!"

"What?" we asked in stereo.

"Well, you know how I wasn't all that excited about taking out a joint last-to-die policy to offset inheritance taxes for Spence and Fraser?"

"Uh-huh," said Rob.

"I really like the idea of making a substantial donation through a life insurance policy. To me, *that* seems like a good use of our money, and of life insurance. But from what Charles is saying, we could have the best of both worlds. We could take out a policy with the death benefit payable to a charity and deduct the premiums from our income taxes now. And then, once we die, the donation credit would offset the tax bill for the kids, at least slightly. Everyone wins!"

"I like it!" said Rob. "I wouldn't mind making that kind of gift to the Alzheimer's society."

"Or the arts centre," said Catherine to Peter. "Maybe we should do the same thing."

"Let's look into it," he said, suppressing a yawn. Seeing him got me started, and soon the five of us were all rubbing our eyes and yawning. It was nearly midnight.

"I think," said Joyce, "that I'm turning in for the night. I'm going to need a good night's sleep to digest all that food — and all that information! Goodnight!"

Recipes for Success

1 Life insurance can be an important part of an estate plan. Used properly, it can minimize the tax burdens upon death.

2 Want to keep the family cottage in the family? One strategy is to buy a life insurance policy that pays the capital gains taxes on the property when its owners die.

3 Parents can consider buying a joint last-to-die policy that pays out on the second death. The kids can use the death benefits to pay the taxes.

4 One in ten Canadians is sixty-five or older! And that figure will quadruple by the 2040s. Long-term-care insurance helps Canadians meet the costs of caring for those who need help with the activities of daily living.

5 It's Patrick! "Guaranteed issue" insurance is an expensive form of permanent insurance designed to cover final expenses, like your funeral. Usually, you don't need to have a medical exam to qualify for it.

6 A life insurance policy can be a great way to make a substantial donation to a charity of your choice. It can also be an effective way to minimize taxes. You can donate a current policy to a charity or make the charity the beneficiary of a policy. You'll receive a donation tax credit for the cash value of the policy and any premiums you pay after donation. Upon your death, the charity receives the death benefit and your estate may receive a tax credit. It's a win-win situation.

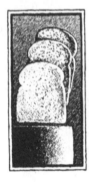

10

UNCLE CHARLES, INC.

*P*OP!

The cork flew out of the champagne bottle and landed somewhere on the grass. Peter poured the fizzy liquid into glasses as we prepared to toast the latest addition to the Stonehouse family — Lindsay and Daniel's week-old baby boy! I looked down at the bundle in my arms and marvelled at the sight of the little one.

"He had good timing," Catherine said. "He wanted to arrive just in time for the Labour Day party."

"My son would never miss a party," said Lindsay.

"Even if he did miss the hospital," said Daniel, shaking his head.

Lindsay's water had broken on August 23, nearly a month earlier than planned, while she was at the school going over some final paperwork with the teacher who would be taking her place during her maternity year. She hadn't told the new gym teacher — just ended the meeting early and headed for home.

"I don't know why you didn't call a cab," Karin had said as Lindsay and Daniel recounted the story earlier that afternoon.

"I felt like walking," said Lindsay. "It was a nice day."

"You're incorrigible," said Lisa, rolling her eyes at her baby sister.

"But by the time I got home, I was soaking! I called Daniel, and he rushed home from his baseball game. Then we called the midwife, who was so calm. She said that she'd be by in a few hours, and that there was plenty of time before we had to go to the hospital, since there were no contractions just yet. So we just opened a bottle of wine and had some dinner and tried to relax."

"And then Lindsay said, 'Hey, I keep getting these little pains in my back every ten minutes or so,'" said Daniel, "and I thought, This baby is coming really soon! So we called the midwife again, and she rushed over. By the time she got there, we could see the baby's head!"

"And there was no way I was going *anywhere* at that point," said Lindsay. "So we ended up having an unplanned home birth! A few hours later, little Charles was here."

I still couldn't quite get over the fact that my niece and nephew-in-law had named their son after me.

"We both liked the name," Lindsay had said to me, "and we also thought that this baby owed you a lot. His future is more secure because of your advice. And maybe," she looked at me and smiled, "he'll turn out like his great-uncle."

Now we stood on the deck, holding glasses of champagne.

"To baby Charles!" announced Peter.

"To baby Charles!" we all echoed, and raised our glasses.

The summer was officially over, an occasion marked by the annual Stonehouse family cottage party. I looked around at my extended family. Peter and Rob were flipping burgers and dogs on the barbecue as Catherine, Joyce, Lisa, and Andrew carried dishes to the picnic table. Lindsay and Daniel were taking a rare opportunity to sit quietly — they hadn't had much sleep in the past week. Fraser had appointed himself bartender, and had gone to get more ice for the cooler. Karin, Spence, and Rebecca were in charge of amusing the kids. Karin and Jack made sandcastles while the other two tossed a Frisbee with Alexandra, Rachel, and Oscar in an abridged game of ultimate. Once I handed back my wee namesake to his new mom, I was designated photographer. I walked about snapping pictures.

"These burgers are ready!" called Peter. "Come and get it!"

We all crowded around the picnic table, which had been set up as a buffet. It was the usual barbecue fare: hotdogs and hamburgers, potato salad, and coleslaw. Simple but delicious.

"Hey, Uncle Charles," said Lisa, "did you make the hamburger buns?"

"Nope, not tonight," I said. "I'm taking a break."

I sat down at a deck chair with my loaded plate and a cold beer. Various nieces and nephews arrayed themselves around me. For a little while, there was no talk, as everyone concentrated on the food. Soon, however, small conversations began to sprout.

"Hey, Uncle Charles," said Karin, "I meant to tell you — I bought disability insurance."

"You did?" I said. "That's great. Where did you end up getting it?"

"Actually, I took your advice and went through my alumni plan. They offer only up to 50 percent of your income in benefits, but it was the most economical coverage available, so I decided to go for it, at least for the time being. I also kept my mortgage insurance for now. I can review it down the line. Thanks for all your advice."

"My pleasure," I said.

"While we're on the subject of insurance," said Lisa, "my partners and I have scheduled a meeting with our accountant in order to get that buy-sell agreement in place. Denise and Lorne really liked the idea."

"Are we still talking insurance?" said Andrew, who had got up for a second burger. He sat down. "Rebecca and I are looking into that universal life policy, Uncle Charles. I told a couple of guys at work about it, and they're pretty gung-ho, too. I should give them your number."

The baby began to fret.

"Obviously, he's tired of all the life insurance talk," I quipped.

"Oh, pass him to me," said Catherine. "Let me hold my newest grandson again."

Lindsay passed little Charles over. Catherine looked beautiful holding the baby. I got up to snap a photo, but the roll was finished. The camera began rewinding.

"I'm going to get more film for my camera," I said, heading for the guest house. Inside, I grabbed a second roll of film and loaded it.

As I returned to the porch, I noticed that it had suddenly got much quieter outside. Peter and Catherine, Joyce and Rob, and my six nieces and nephews and their families stood in a semicircle, grinning.

"What are you doing?" I asked.

"We have an announcement for you, Uncle Charles," said Lindsay.

"Really?" I said. "What else could there possibly be?"

"Well," said Karin, "we wanted to thank you for all the help you've given to us over the summer. We all learned so much from you, and we wanted to give something back. So . . ." She looked around and signalled to Jack, Alexandra, Rachel, and Oscar, who were off to one side, giggling. The kids came forward and handed me a large envelope.

"Open it!" demanded Alex.

I did. Inside there was a beautiful card, signed by my siblings and my nieces and nephews. My great-nieces and -nephews had carefully printed their names, and Lindsay and Daniel had dipped baby Charles's foot in ink and added his "signature" — a tiny footprint — as well. The card thanked me for my "valuable and loving life insurance advice," and for my "wonderful bread." The envelope also included a gift certificate — for a twelve-week introductory class at a gourmet cooking school in Kingston!

My eyes misted.

"This is wonderful," I said. "Completely unnecessary, but wonderful. Thank you."

"We thought it was time you branched out," explained Andrew. "I mean, there's a whole world of food out there besides bread."

"Maybe next year I'll spend the summer here and cook gourmet meals for you all every night," I said.

"Fine with me!" said Peter.

"Me too," said Catherine. "I expect that we'll have a lot more visitors if that's the case."

"I guess I have an announcement to make, too," I said, looking around at my extended family. "I've decided what I'm going to do in my retirement — at least, when I'm not cooking gourmet meals."

"Do tell," said Peter.

"Well, I've had such a good time conducting Uncle Charles's Life Insurance Seminars all summer that I think I want to continue to do it. Why not put together a series of seminars for community colleges to educate people on life insurance? I could do group seminars and counsel people individually, too. Who knows? Maybe one day I could even write a book about it!"

"That's a great idea!" said Lindsay. "I know tons of people who could use your advice. Lots of my colleagues at work, for example. You could go into schools for professional development seminars!"

"I can design your web site, Uncle Charles," said Fraser.

"And I can write the copy for it," added Karin.

"I could . . . be the technical consultant or something," added Lisa. "Anything to help."

"I love it!" said Joyce. "You'll have to come to Toronto and do a series of seminars there. We'll put you up."

"Come to Montreal, too," said Andrew.

"And Ottawa," added Daniel.

"I can just see it," said Lindsay, shifting her new son in her arms. "A world tour! And it all started here, at this cottage."

"Quite astounding, isn't it?" I said. "Actually, I guess we could say that little Charles here was the inspiration for all of this. May I?"

Lindsay passed the squirming bundle over to me, and I looked into the tiny, red face.

Peter cleared his throat. "I propose a toast," he said. "To Charles's second career: gourmet chef and insurance seminar conductor par excellence!"

"To Uncle Charles, Incorporated!" said Catherine, raising her glass.

"To Uncle Charles, Incorporated," echoed my family.

Appendix A:

Needs Analysis

Step 1:

Calculate how much income your survivors
will need **each month**.

Food	$ _____
Clothing	$ _____
Housing:	
Rent (mortgages discussed below)	$ _____
Property taxes	$ _____
Utilities	$ _____
Insurance premiums	$ _____
Home maintenance and repair	$ _____
Transportation:	
Public transit	$ _____
Car lease	$ _____
Car insurance, licence	$ _____
Car maintenance	$ _____
Education	$ _____
Child care	$ _____

Investments:

Life insurance premiums	$ _____
RRSP contributions	$ _____
RESP contributions	$ _____
Other investments	$ _____
Vacations and Entertainment	$ _____
Other: _____	$ _____
_____	$ _____

TOTAL   (A) $ _____

Step 2:

To find out your survivors'
annual income needs, multiply your
monthly needs (A) by 12:   (B) $ _____

Step 3:

To find out your **annual shortfall**, calculate
your survivors' current **annual** sources of
income, plus any government benefits.

Salary (annual)	$ _____
Canada/Quebec Pension Plan benefits	$ _____
Survivor benefits	$ _____
Orphan benefits	$ _____
Interest and investment income	$ _____
Employment insurance	$ _____
Other sources of income	$ _____

TOTAL   (C) $ _____

Subtract **(C)** from **(B)**:
(B) $ _____ − **(C)** $ _____ = **(D)** $ _____

This is your annual shortfall. If (D) is a
negative number, calculate it as zero (0).

Step 4:

Calculate your **immediate,
lump-sum expenses and debts**.

Final expenses (funeral, burial)	$ _____
Mortgage(s)	
(unless you have mortgage insurance)	$ _____
Loans (car, student, business, personal)	$ _____
Legal/probate fees	$ _____
Business expenses	$ _____
Medical bills	$ _____
Income taxes	$ _____
Credit card debt	$ _____
Other debt: _____	$ _____
_____	$ _____

TOTAL (E) $ _____

Step 5:

Calculate any **future lump-sum expenses**,
such as a new car or children's university
education.

Car	$ _____
University education tuition fees	$ _____
Other future expenses	$ _____

TOTAL (F) $ _____

Step 6:

Calculate the amount of life insurance
coverage you'll need.

6A. Divide your annual shortfall (**D**) by
6% (or 0.06; conservative),
8% (or 0.08; less conservative), or
10% (or 0.1; optimistic) to calculate your
future capital needs. (If your annual
shortfall is zero, go to step **6B**.)

(**D**) $ _____ x [0.06 or 0.08 or 0.1] = (**G**) $ _____

6B. Add:
Future capital needs (**G**): $ _____
Immediate lump-sum expenses
    and debts (**E**):   + $ _____
Future lump-sum expenses (**F**):   + $ _____

TOTAL = $ _____

Subtract any life insurance coverage
you may already have through group
and other insurance plans.   – $ _____

TOTAL = $ _____

This is approximately the amount of life insurance
coverage you need today. Remember, each spouse/partner
in a relationship will need to do his or her own calculation.
This needs analysis does not take into account inflation,
which will magnify your life insurance needs over time.
For a detailed analysis of your insurance needs, contact
a qualified financail advisor.

Appendix B:

For Further Research

Web Sites

For information on disability and survivor benefits:

Human Resources Development Canada
www.hrdc-drhc.gc.ca/isp.common/cpptoc_e.shtml

Books

Cestnick, Tim. *Winning the Tax Game: A Year-Round Tax and Investment Guide for Canadians.* Toronto: Prentice Hall, 1988.

Chilton, David. *The Wealthy Barber: The Common Sense Guide to Successful Financial Planning.* Toronto: Stoddart Publishing, 1989.

Cork, David, and Susan Lightstone. *The Pig and the Python: How to Prosper from the Aging Baby Boom.* Toronto: Stoddart Publishing, 1996.

Associations and Organizations

Canadian Association of Insurance and Financial Advisors (CAIFA)

CAIFA is a professional association that represents insurance and financial advisors across Canada. It provides referrals and free consumer information on choosing insurance and financial advisors, life insurance, and a range of related products.

350 Bloor Street East, 2nd Floor
Toronto, ON M4W 3W8
Tel: (416) 444-5251
Toll-free: 1-800-563-5822
e-mail: info@caifa.com
www.caifa.com

Canadian Life and Health Insurance Association (CLHIA), Consumer Assistance Centre

The CLHIA is a trade association representing about ninety life and health insurers. It operates a Consumer Assistance Centre, a source of information and assistance to Canadian consumers of insurance.

Suite 1700, 1 Queen Street East
Toronto, ON M5C 2X9
For information in English, call: 1-800-268-8099 (in Toronto, call: (416) 777-2344).
Pour renseignements en français, téléphonez: 1-800-361-8070 (en Montréal, téléphonez: (514) 845-6173).
e-mail: CAC@clhia.ca
www.clhia.ca/e7.htm

The Canadian Life and Health Insurance Compensation Corporation (COMPCORP)

e-mail: info@compcorp.ca

www.compcorp.ca

Financial Planners Standards Council (FPSC)

The Financial Planners Standards Council benefits the public and the financial planning profession by establishing and enforcing competency and ethical standards for financial planners who choose to hold this internationally recognized professional designation: CFP. Check their web site for a list of members.

505 University Avenue

Suite 1600

Toronto, ON M5G 1X3

Tel: (416) 593-8587

Toll-free: 1-800-305-9886

Fax: (416) 593-6903

e-mail: inform@cfp-ca.org

www.cfp-ca.org

About the Authors

Paul Grimes is a veteran of the insurance industry. In the twenty years he's been in the business, he's done it all, from knocking on doors to sell individual policies, to designing new life insurance products and managing the integration of two large insurance companies. Today, Paul is Ontario vice-president of sales for Industrial Alliance, one of Canada's leading life insurance companies. He is a certified financial planner, a chartered life underwriter, and a chartered financial consultant. His dynamic and personable speaking style makes him a sought-after speaker on sales techniques, life and health insurance, and financial planning.

Paul has advised hundreds of Canadian families and businesses on their life and group health insurance needs. He knows the insurance industry inside out, and he's put that knowledge to work in *The Facts of Life*, using his vast experience to guide Canadians through an increasingly complex market. His insider's knowledge will provide readers with the confidence they need to make informed decisions about life insurance. He lives in Toronto with his wife, Denise, and sons, Fraser and Spencer.

Susan Goldberg is an award-winning freelance writer and editor, whose work has appeared in a variety of Canadian publications. She lives in Toronto.